D1607508

Divorce For Men

A Self-Help Book to Reclaim Your Strength, Rediscover Your Purpose, and Create a Life Worth Living After the Divorce

Ethan Crosswell

Contents

Introduction

"When we are no longer able to change a situation, we are challenged to change ourselves." – Viktor Frankl

"I never thought this would be my story."

That was me, finally letting it all out like an overinflated balloon that couldn't take another puff. Those words spilled out one night as I sat in my half-empty apartment, staring at a sad little pile of boxes—a pathetic monument to the demise of my marriage. Saying it out loud didn't lighten the load; it just made the truth punch harder. But hey, every miserable journey starts with a single, cringeworthy step.

At that time, my life was in a mess, one I hadn't anticipated or prepared for. My marriage had ended, and the future I thought was certain had become clouded with uncertainty. No, I never imagined myself to be a divorcee. I didn't want this life and didn't choose it. Yet, there I was, facing a reality I couldn't change.

If you're reading this book, you're feeling the same way. You feel hurt, forsaken, disappointed, and abandoned. Maybe you're sitting alone in a room that used to feel warm and full of life but now feels cold and unfamiliar. Or perhaps you're staring at a bank statement, wondering how to make ends meet. Like me, you've possibly looked in the mirror and struggled to recognize the person staring back.

Divorce is like a storm that leaves no part of your life untouched. It floods your emotions, uproots your plans, and casts clouds of uncertainty over your future. The thunder of arguments echoes in your mind, and the downpour of grief seems endless, soaking every aspect of your life in its weight. It shakes your confidence, muddles your mind, and leaves you questioning everything. It challenges your identity, plans, and even your sense of worth. The life you envisioned now feels like a distant dream, replaced by a painful struggle to make sense of your entire existence.

Amid the chaos lies a small and persistent voice—perhaps it's hope, a spark of inner strength, or even a whisper of intuition—letting you know that this isn't where your story ends. At least that voice has led you to read this book, which promises to be life-changing.

Psychiatrist and author Victor Frankl's words, "When we are no longer able to change a situation, we are challenged to change ourselves," offer a powerful reminder. While you can't change the fact that your marriage has ended or erase the arguments, mistakes, or pain, you have the power to decide how you respond to it. Divorce doesn't have to be the final chapter of your story. Instead, see it as a turning point and a chance to rewrite your narrative and uncover the possibilities that lie beyond the pain you feel.

I remember waking up many nights, staring at the ceiling, my mind racing with "what-ifs" and regrets. And, of course, those trips to the bathroom at 3 a.m. didn't help—just another reminder of how sleepless and restless I'd become. "Is this who I am now?" I'd ask myself. The question hung in the air, unanswered. In the morning, I'd wake up feeling hopeless, drained, and exhausted even when I hadn't lifted a finger.

Perhaps you've had moments like that. Maybe you now feel awkward in social settings where everyone knows your story or struggle with the unfamiliar silence that fills your home after your kids leave for their other parent's house. It can be hard to stay composed when someone gives misguided advice like, "Don't worry, you'll be fine in no time."

The truth is, no two divorces are the same. For some, the process unfolds quietly, with minimal conflict and little to dwell on. For others, it's loud and chaotic, filled with sleepless nights, bitter arguments, and exhausting court battles. Whichever your experience is, the emotional weight of divorce is heavy. It doesn't matter how it happened; the pain is real, and it deserves to be acknowledged.

It's okay to grieve. In fact, it's necessary to grieve before healing. Grieving is a process, and it often comes in waves. You may feel denial one day, anger the next, and sadness after that. Healthy grieving might look like allowing yourself to cry, seeking support from trusted friends or a therapist, or finding ways to honor the past while focusing on the future. Remember, it's not a race—it's a journey unique to you. Divorce can be considered a loss, and with any loss, there's a period of mourning. However, there should also be hope. As your divorce marks the end of a chapter, be hopeful that you have a chance to rewrite your narrative and rediscover who you are as an individual.

So why did I write this book? Because I've been where you are now. In my dark moments, I wished I had someone to guide me, letting me know that I wasn't alone and I'd get through this. I needed to know that while a chapter of my life was closing, it didn't mean that my story was over. This book will serve as a reminder for you. It's a resource born out of my personal experience, struggles, and growth.

I am sharing what I've learned, not as an expert but as someone who's been where you are, made the same mistakes and learned from them, wrestled with the same doubts and fears, and come out the other side stronger and more self-assured.

Healing takes time and patience, but it's possible. This book doesn't minimize your feelings or preach that healing is easy. It acknowledges the messiness of divorce, offers tools to navigate it, and reminds you that there is hope, even when it feels out of reach.

As you read this book, reflect on your journey. What brought you to this point? What emotions are you carrying? What hopes or fears keep you awake at night? These questions aren't easy to answer, especially now, but they're worth exploring. They'll serve as a foundation for rebuilding your life. Don't blame yourself or dwell on regrets; the goal is to find clarity and set the stage for what comes next.

This book will guide you from the raw pain of loss to a life of renewed hope and joy. We'll start by addressing the emotional, mental, and physical shifts that follow the end of a marriage. You'll confront the realities of grief and social stigma while learning to process your feelings authentically and recognizing that healing doesn't follow a straight path. From there, we'll focus on building emotional resilience, rediscovering your self-worth, and setting a purposeful vision for your future. The goal is to empower you to reclaim control over your life.

As you progress, you'll learn practical strategies for rebuilding your relationships, regaining financial and physical stability, and avoiding common recovery pitfalls that can hinder your growth. By the end, you'll move from merely surviving to genuinely finding joy and purpose while building connections with others who've walked a similar path.

This process won't be easy. There will be days when moving forward seems impossible. But there will also be moments of joy reminding you of your strength.

You've already taken the first step by reading this book. Now, let this be the beginning of a journey where you reclaim your strength, embrace your resilience, and take bold steps toward building a brighter future. Ready to get started? Stay with me.

Chapter One

The Reality of Divorce:

What You're Really Going Through

"In the middle of every difficulty lies opportunity."

- Albert Einstein

The Reality of Divorce

According to studies by the American Psychological Association (APA), approximately 40-50% of first marriages in the United States end in divorce, though this rate has been declining slightly over recent years. Behind those numbers lie many dreams that have been shattered, futures completely rewritten, and lives turned upside down.

At 42, I found myself becoming one of those statistics. The numbers had always felt distant, just abstract figures that had nothing to do with me—until suddenly, they did. I had just gotten out of a 10-year marriage, and my life was a complete mess. It felt like I had hit rock bottom as everything I thought I knew and had planned for was crumbling right before my eyes. I was hopeless, overwhelmed, and unable to move forward.

Every morning, I'd wake up with a weight on my chest so heavy it felt like it might crush me. No matter what I did, the dread remained. When I looked in the mirror, I didn't recognize the man staring back at me. That wasn't the man I imagined I'd grow into or the man I'd worked so hard to become. The man staring back was tired, beaten down, and a shadow of someone I once knew.

The Weight of Shame

The strongest emotion I felt was shame. I was ashamed of my failures, the mistakes I couldn't undo, and the person I feared I'd become. The thoughts running through my head were relentless: *Why am I not good enough? Why does everything I touch fall apart? Will I ever escape this darkness?* These questions echoed in my mind, feeding an endless cycle of self-doubt and despair that seemed impossible to break.

The cycle continued for months, each day blending into the next, until I had a turning point. One day, while aimlessly reading articles, I stumbled upon a quote by Albert Einstein: *"In the middle of every difficulty lies opportunity."* At first, I scoffed. *What opportunity could possibly come from the wreckage of my marriage? How could there be anything positive in this unbearable mess?* However, Einstein's words stuck with me. In my quiet moments, when I was left alone with my thoughts, they haunted me.

Over time, I realized that Einstein wasn't saying the difficulty itself was an opportunity. Instead, he meant that hardship can serve as a catalyst for transformation. It's not about continuing the past—it's about using adversity as a foundation for something entirely new.

Beyond the Legal Process

Divorce is more than a legal event. I remember sitting in the courtroom, the sound of the judge's gavel sealing the end of my marriage. It was supposed to bring closure, but instead, I felt a hollow ache in my chest. The legal proceedings were just a formality—the real battle was the emotional turmoil that followed. Divorce shakes your very core, leaving you exposed, vulnerable, and searching for stability. It affects your physical body, mental state, emotions, and even your social relationships. You may feel isolated, as though no one truly understands the grief you're experiencing.

For me, the grief was overwhelming. I experienced anger, sadness, guilt, and even denial. The experience was unpredictable to the extent that I constantly doubted whether I could ever put the pieces of my life back together.

A New Perspective

Through reflection and self-discovery, I've come to realize that divorce isn't the end of my story. It's just a chapter—unexpected and unwanted, but temporary. Despite how painful it is, we need to see it as a chance to rewrite our narrative and rebuild our lives on our own terms. With the right mindset and the willingness to face the pain head-on, you'll see that even in the darkest moments, there is power in choosing to move forward.

What's Ahead

This first chapter is about helping you make sense of what you're going through. We'll discuss the emotional, mental, and physical toll divorce takes on you, acknowledging your challenges. We'll also explore the grief that comes with divorce, not as a linear process but as a deeply personal journey that unfolds differently for everyone. The goal isn't to rush you through the pain or offer false promises of instant healing. Instead, it's to let you know that even when life feels shattered, you have the power to rebuild.

Understanding Emotional, Mental, and Physical Shifts

The Moment of Realization

It wasn't a sudden realization but a slow, creeping awareness that settled in over time. I remember when it finally dawned on me that my marriage had ended. At first, I found myself overwhelmed by the complexity of my situation. I recall sitting in my car for hours after a difficult conversation with my ex-wife, staring at the steering wheel, unsure whether I should cry, scream, or drive aimlessly until I ran out of gas. In that moment, it wasn't just the loss of the relationship that I was mourning—it was the future I had envisioned, the life I thought I'd have.

After that realization, I knew my life was changing in more ways than I had anticipated. There is no sugarcoating it; divorce is more than a legal separation. It is a life-altering event that affects you on every level. It's like a storm that sweeps through your world, leaving behind emotional chaos, mental exhaustion, and even physical strain. To truly understand these changes and help regain balance, let's explore the emotional, mental, and physical shifts that come with divorce.

Emotional Shifts

Have you noticed that after your divorce, you've been feeling angry, betrayed, sad, guilty, or resentful? One moment, you feel okay, maybe even relieved, and the next, you're drowning in a wave of emotions, wishing you could hide from the world. Divorce triggers a rollercoaster of emotions, shaking the very foundation of your identity.

One of the most challenging aspects is grief—not just for the relationship, but for the future you and your ex once envisioned. Dreams of shared milestones, routines, and traditions are now gone. Then comes the anger, directed at your ex, at fate, and even at yourself. You may find yourself asking, *Could I have done more? Was this my fault?*

I remember one Saturday morning when I sat alone at the breakfast table. Saturdays used to be filled with laughter and pancakes. Now, silence filled the room, a weekly reminder of what I had lost.

Divorce also brings an unexpected loss of identity. You're no longer part of a "we"—you're figuring out how to be just *you* again. The collateral damage extends beyond the relationship itself, affecting friendships and family connections tied to your marriage. These secondary losses can deepen feelings of loneliness, making it even harder to move forward.

The grief of losing a marriage is real, even if your relationship was far from perfect.

Mental Shifts

Do you find yourself caught in a cycle of overthinking and self-doubt? Replaying arguments? Wondering how things could have been different? Divorce can consume your mind with endless "what-ifs," making it difficult to focus on the present or see a way forward.

The mental toll of divorce doesn't stop with decision paralysis. It can deeply affect your self-worth. Thoughts like, *Why wasn't I enough? Who am I without my partner? Will I ever be happy again?* become common.

I remember one day at the grocery store, standing in the cereal aisle, completely paralyzed. The task was simple—buy cereal. Yet, I stood there, staring at the shelves, unable to make a choice. It wasn't about the cereal; it was about the overwhelming changes in my life bleeding into the smallest moments.

Chronic stress activates your brain's fight-or-flight response, flooding your body with stress hormones like cortisol. Over time, this impairs your ability to think clearly, focus, or even remember simple things. It can also lead to anxiety and depression if left unchecked.

Physical Shifts

After experiencing the emotional highs and lows and the mental exhaustion that divorce brings, your body begins to feel the weight of it all. Just as divorce affects your emotions and mind, it also takes a toll on your body in ways you might not immediately recognize. Stress from divorce can manifest physically in ways you wouldn't expect. Sleep disturbances are common—nights filled with tossing and turning, replaying past conversations, and worrying about the future.

Stress-related ailments soon follow: muscle tension, constant headaches, and digestive issues. Another overlooked symptom is the impact on your appetite. While some find comfort in food, leading to weight gain, others lose their appetite entirely.

The lack of sleep was the hardest part for me. Many nights, I'd lie awake, staring at the ceiling, unable to quiet my thoughts. One morning, I woke up on the living room couch, still in the clothes I had worn the day before. I didn't even remember falling asleep there. The exhaustion had caught up with me. That moment made me realize I had to address not just my emotional pain but also the toll it was taking on my body.

Scientific research shows that chronic stress—like that caused by divorce—can have long-term health effects, increasing the risk of high blood pressure, heart disease, and a weakened immune system. That's why self-care during this time isn't a luxury—it's a necessity.

Steps Toward Healing

While these emotional, mental, and physical shifts are overwhelming, they are also signals that you are human. To regain your footing and start healing, consider these practical strategies:

1. Acknowledge Your Feelings

Your emotions won't disappear just because you ignore them. Instead of suppressing them, try journaling or talking to a trusted friend or professional. Grieving isn't a sign of failure—it's a natural response to loss.

2. Reclaim Mental Clarity

Simplify your decisions. When everything feels overwhelming, break things down into small, manageable steps. Start your day by asking yourself, *What's one thing I can do today?* Mindfulness exercises, like deep breathing, can also help calm your mind and reduce stress.

3. Prioritize Physical Self-Care

Even if sleep feels impossible right now, establish a routine. Limit screen time before bed, create a calm environment, and make movement a part of your day. A short walk or gentle exercise can help release stress and boost your mood.

Through my divorce, I've learned that while the process is undeniably painful, it's also an opportunity for transformation. It forced me to confront parts of myself I had neglected and to rebuild my identity from the ground up. In that process, I discovered a resilience I never knew I had.

If you feel like you're drowning right now, know that you aren't alone, and the storm won't last forever. Hold on, take one step at a time, and trust that with each passing day, you are moving closer to healing and rediscovering your strength. Yes, healing takes time, but you are already taking small steps toward finding yourself again.

Navigating the Social Stigma of Divorce

The Weight of Judgment

The shame attached to the 'divorce' label only deepened my pain. It wasn't just the loss of my partner that hurt, but also the fear of how others would perceive me. Imagine the hardest part of my divorce not being the fact that I had lost my partner, but the fear of being "the divorced guy" everyone had an opinion about. I remember walking into a friend's engagement party, and as soon as I entered, the air seemed to shift. Eyes darted in my direction, conversations hushed, and even my well-meaning friends seemed unsure of what to say. My divorce didn't just affect me in private—it made me feel like a public spectacle. I felt like a label I never asked for was stamped on my forehead.

The social stigma attached to divorce makes it feel even more isolating. Many people will pass judgment, offer unsolicited advice, or treat you differently. Some may not mean to act that way or may not even be aware of their actions. Certain words will sting, but I later realized that their opinions weren't about me. They were reflections of their own fears or beliefs about marriage and failure, not mine. I recognized that I wasn't living for the approval of others but for my own future.

Understanding and addressing social stigmas is crucial to maintaining self-worth during a difficult time. The following are some of the most common stigmas surrounding divorce and how they can affect your self-perception.

The Guilt of Being "The One Who Left"

Divorce is already hard enough, and if you were the one who initiated it, the weight of guilt might feel unbearable. During my experience, people around me had opinions: "Did he really try hard enough?" or "Was there no way to fix it?" It was as if the end of my marriage had given others the license to question my integrity and commitment.

But what others didn't see were the quiet battles I fought behind closed doors—the sleepless nights, the endless arguments, and the tears I shed trying to hold on to what was already gone. They didn't witness the moments I sat on the edge of my bed, questioning whether I was making the right decision or dealing with the overwhelming fear of the unknown.

If you're feeling this guilt, remind yourself that your choice wasn't made lightly. Practice self-compassion and acknowledge that choosing your well-being is not selfish—it's necessary. Recognizing your own needs and valuing your happiness is an act of courage, not failure. Divorce isn't about "giving up" but about choosing what's best for your well-being. Staying in an unhappy or toxic relationship doesn't make you a hero—it makes you a prisoner. Strength lies in knowing when to walk away, and that's okay.

The Pressure of Expectations

Many people see divorce as a failure, a broken promise, or even a symbol of weakness. Society often idolizes the idea of "forever," and when a marriage ends, it's easy to feel like you've let everyone down. In one conversation, I remember a family friend saying, "I thought you two were perfect together. What happened?" She meant well, but her words still felt like a dagger to my heart.

The weight of such expectations can be crushing. You start questioning yourself: *What did I do wrong? Why couldn't I make it work?* But the truth is, relationships end for many reasons. Some marriages face irreconcilable differences, others are under external pressures, and some simply run their course. Whatever the reason, it doesn't make you a failure. Don't let societal expectations dictate how you view yourself. A marriage ending isn't the end of your worth—it's the closing of one chapter, making room for a new beginning.

Dealing with Friends and Family

Even when friends and family mean well, they can sometimes add to the burden you already carry. My parents, heartbroken over my divorce, unintentionally made things harder for me. When I was trying to move on, my mom would say things like, "Couldn't you have tried one more time?" while my dad barely spoke about it. His silence felt heavy with disappointment.

Beyond my immediate family, some friends felt compelled to take sides. Some drifted away, unsure how to fit into the changed dynamic, while others offered well-meaning but unhelpful advice like, "Just move on" or "You'll find someone else soon."

I had to set boundaries to ensure my peace. I knew I didn't owe anyone an explanation for my decisions or my pain. Instead, I leaned on those who supported me—the ones who listened without judgment, who held space for my feelings, and who reminded me I wasn't alone. Setting these boundaries wasn't easy, but it became necessary for my healing. For instance, I stopped engaging in conversations that left me feeling drained and instead prioritized relationships that made me feel supported. Creating this space allowed me to focus on rebuilding my confidence and embracing a healthier mindset.

Rebuilding Your Identity

I've mentioned losing your identity and the need to rebuild it throughout this book. So, why is it so important? If you were once half of a couple, you might now feel unsure about who you are as an individual.

As a couple, I did many things with my partner, but suddenly, it was just me. Attending events where we used to go together felt awkward and daunting. Over time, though, I saw the opportunity in this change. I now had the chance to rediscover who I was outside of marriage. *What makes me happy? What do I want from life?* I asked myself questions I hadn't considered in years.

I remember signing up for a gym class. It was a small step, but one that reminded me how much I loved working out. I started taking weekend hikes, reconnecting with nature, and spending time with myself. These activities weren't about "finding myself" in a cliché sense—they were about embracing parts of me that I had neglected while focusing on being someone else's partner.

It takes time to rediscover your identity, but every step is worth it. You are a whole person, capable of happiness and growth. Don't be defined by your relationship status.

Moving Past the Stigma

The social stigma of divorce won't disappear overnight, but you can change how it affects you. Instead of seeing yourself as a failure, see your divorce as a sign of courage—a recognition of what wasn't working and a commitment to pursue a better life.

There will be times when judgment from others feels heavy, when whispers and disapproving glances sting. But remember that those opinions don't define you. Don't dwell on them; choose to move forward.

Surround yourself with people who uplift you, who celebrate your journey instead of questioning it. The focus now is to build a life that reflects your passions, values, and dreams. When in doubt or feeling insecure, remind yourself that you aren't less capable, less worthy, or less deserving of happiness.

Navigating the social stigma of divorce can be daunting, but it also presents an invaluable opportunity for self-growth, healing, and transformation. Instead of viewing it as a burden, embrace it as a turning point—a chance to rediscover your strength, reclaim your identity, and build a future that aligns with your true self. The next time someone's opinion threatens to overshadow your journey, take a deep breath and remember: your worth is tied to the person you're becoming—the one facing the pain, rising above judgment, and forging a new path forward.

Acknowledging the Stages of Grief

Grief is often associated with loss, but it's not just about death. It can also be tied to the end of relationships, including divorce. Traditionally, grief is broken down into five stages: denial, anger, bargaining, depression, and acceptance. While these stages provide a useful framework, they don't always follow a linear path. Grief isn't a clean step-by-step process; it's deeply personal, messy, and unpredictable. You may find yourself revisiting certain stages even after thinking you had moved past them, and that's completely normal. Healing isn't about following a straight path—it's about learning to navigate the twists and turns along the way. Sometimes, you'll skip stages, revisit one, or experience them in a completely different order. This is normal because we all grieve differently.

Understanding the five stages of grief can help you make sense of overwhelming emotions and reassure you that your feelings are valid.

1. Denial

At first, you might find it hard to accept that your marriage is truly over. This stage can feel like you're stuck in a fog, unable or unwilling to confront the reality of your situation. For me, I tried convincing myself that the separation was temporary, that we just needed space to cool off. I replayed our last conversations over and over, searching for clues that everything would go back to the way it was. That was me living in denial.

Denial is your mind's way of shielding you from the impact of loss. It's a form of emotional self-preservation that, though temporary, gives you some time to process the reality of your situation. During this phase, you might find yourself asking questions like, "Did I do enough?" or "Could I have saved this?"

No doubt, denial can provide short-term comfort, serving as a temporary buffer against pain. However, it's essential to acknowledge that while denial is a natural response, true healing comes from facing reality and working through the emotions that follow. Eventually, the truth seeps in, often in painful doses. It could be the day you pack up the last box of your belongings from the home you shared with your ex or when you start dividing assets. The emptiness of those moments forces you to confront the reality you've been avoiding.

2. Anger

As the fog of denial lifts, anger often follows. Anger can be overwhelming, surfacing in unexpected ways and at unexpected moments. It may be directed at your ex, yourself, or even life itself.

When I reached this phase, I was furious about things I once saw as trivial. *Why didn't my ex fight harder for our marriage? Why did our friends seem to pick sides? Why did life feel so unfair?* I asked myself these questions repeatedly.

Anger is a natural response to feeling betrayed, misunderstood, or hurt. It's a way of pushing back against the vulnerability grief brings. The mistake many grieving individuals make—including myself—is seeing anger as an enemy. But anger is not the enemy; it's a powerful emotion that demands attention. Suppressing it can lead to bitterness, while acknowledging and expressing it can clear the path to healing.

When I was overwhelmed by rage, I turned to exercise. Short walks, long runs, and workouts became my therapy. With each step, I released some of the pent-up frustration inside me. The goal isn't to stay angry but to process the emotion in healthy ways. In addition to exercise, activities like journaling, meditation, or talking with a trusted friend can help release frustration and provide clarity.

3. Bargaining

This stage is a natural part of trying to make sense of things or wishing for a way out of the pain. Bargaining often involves making deals with yourself or the universe. It's a mental game of "what if" and "if only." *If only I had been more patient... If only we had gone to therapy sooner...*

At this phase, my bargaining was fueled by regret. I replayed arguments, wondering if I could have said or done something differently. I clung to the hope that maybe, just maybe, there was still a way to fix things with my ex. Over time, I learned to shift my perspective. Instead of focusing on what I could have done differently, I started asking myself what I could learn from the experience and how I could grow.

Bargaining is a sign that you're actively engaging with your grief, even if it feels like you're running in circles. It's emotionally exhausting, as it forces you to confront the "what could have been" scenarios that rarely have clear answers. While this stage can feel never-ending, it's also a step toward healing.

4. Depression

As the reality of your divorce sets in, depression often follows. This stage isn't just about sadness; it involves a sense of loss, loneliness, and hopelessness. You might feel exhausted, overwhelmed, and disconnected from the world around you.

Depression was the hardest stage for me. There were days when getting out of bed felt impossible. I withdrew from friends and family, convinced that no one truly understood what I was going through. Even small tasks, like checking my emails, felt difficult.

This stage can be isolating, but it's also a necessary part of healing. Depression, like all stages of grief, is temporary. It might feel endless in the moment, but with time and support, the heaviness begins to lift. Acknowledge your pain without letting it consume you. Seek support from friends, family, or professionals who can help you navigate these feelings.

5. Acceptance

I remember the moment I realized I had reached acceptance. I was sitting alone on a Saturday morning, drinking coffee and reading a book, when it hit me: I was okay. The life I had envisioned with my ex was no longer my reality, but that didn't mean I couldn't create a new one. I was ready to move forward.

Acceptance is when you begin to find peace with your new reality. It doesn't mean you're happy about the divorce or that you've forgotten the pain—it means you are ready to move forward. Acceptance doesn't erase the hurt; it allows you to stop dwelling on the past.

Be Kind to Yourself

Grieving the end of your marriage can be one of the most challenging experiences you'll face. Regardless of the pain, be patient with yourself. Don't rush through the stages of healing as if they were items on a checklist. Honor your emotions and give yourself the time and space to recover.

Surround yourself with people who lift you up and remind you of your strength, whether it's friends, family, or a therapist. When the days feel especially hard, remind yourself that you're not alone. Countless others have faced similar struggles and emerged stronger. You will too.

Embrace the ups and downs, knowing they are stepping stones to recovery. Healing is an ongoing journey, not a destination. There will be setbacks, but each moment of struggle is an opportunity for growth. Over time, the weight will become lighter, and you'll emerge stronger. It's okay not to have everything figured out right away. As you continue this journey, you'll begin to see the possibility of a future where the pain of the past no longer holds you back.

Chapter Key Points:

- Divorce impacts every aspect of life—emotional, mental, and physical. Recognizing these shifts can help you navigate them.

- Society often labels divorce as a failure, leading to feelings of shame or isolation. These judgments are reflections of others' perceptions, not your reality.

- Grieving a divorce is not a linear process. Acknowledge your unique journey and be kind to yourself as you heal.

- While divorce feels like an ending, it also marks a new beginning. This chapter encourages self-reflection and empowers you to embrace your future with confidence.

Chapter Two

Reclaiming Your Power:

Building Emotional Resilience

"Do not pray foran easy life, pray for the strength to endure a difficult one."
- Bruce Lee

Rebuilding Your Self-Worth After Divorce

Why does divorce hurt so badly? Why does it hit so hard and shake your very core? What is it about the experience that makes you question all your choices, identity, and the road ahead?

Divorce is more than just the loss of a partner—it's the dismantling of a life you once knew. According to the Holmes-Rahe Stress Scale, divorce is ranked as one of the most stressful life events, second only to the death of a spouse. Unlike death, which has finality, divorce forces you to live with painful memories, unresolved emotions, and sometimes ongoing interactions with your ex. These ongoing interactions can be emotionally draining, making it harder to heal fully. Whether it's co-parenting, mutual social circles, or shared financial responsibilities, each encounter can reopen wounds, forcing you to navigate complex emotions repeatedly. Learning how to manage these interactions in a way that protects your emotional well-being is crucial for moving forward.

One moment, your life feels predictable, and the next, it feels like it has been turned upside down. You're forced to confront who you are without the relationship that once defined you. You'll face the fear of an uncertain future, the pressure of rediscovering yourself, and the overwhelming weight of emotional baggage.

The Path to Emotional Resilience

While the emotional rollercoaster you're on right now feels endless, there's hope. Despite your experience, you can build emotional resilience. This doesn't mean erasing your pain or pretending certain things didn't happen. It means reclaiming your power and learning to control your emotions in ways that put you back on track. The end of your marriage isn't the end of who you are or who you can become.

When my marriage ended, I was devastated—not just because I had lost a partner I had lived with for over ten years, but because I had lost everything I thought I knew about myself. The emotions I felt in those early days were overwhelming. I remember waking up in the middle of the night, my heart pounding, feeling like I had lost my sense of identity. The silence of the empty house was deafening, a constant reminder of what was missing. Simple tasks, like making coffee or folding laundry, became unbearable as they were steeped in memories of a life I no longer had. The weight of it all made it hard to breathe, and for a while, I wondered if I would ever feel normal again.

But along the way, I had to give myself a wake-up call. "What's the worst that could happen?" I asked myself. I knew the worst thing would be letting my emotions control and consume me, which had happened for too long. I needed a change. I didn't need to ignore or suppress my feelings—I needed to learn how to manage them. This is where emotional resilience comes in.

Building emotional resilience means facing your emotions head-on, learning to understand them, and finding healthier ways to cope. With resilience, when you get knocked down, you can get back up, stronger and wiser. I remember a time when I had to attend a family gathering shortly after my divorce. The thought of facing people who knew me as part of a couple felt unbearable. But instead of avoiding it, I went. It wasn't easy, and

I felt moments of sadness, but I also realized my ability to engage in conversations, find support, and remind myself that I was more than my past relationship. That experience showed me that resilience isn't just about bouncing back—it's about stepping forward, even when it feels difficult.

The Role of Self-Awareness and Self-Worth

During my divorce, confronting how I saw myself was one of the most difficult challenges. My divorce shook the foundation of everything I thought I knew about myself, leaving me feeling lost and disconnected. However, through self-awareness and self-worth, I was able to rediscover who I was and stay grounded.

Self-awareness involves reflecting on who you are, your strengths and weaknesses, and how your actions align with your values. It's the ability to understand yourself mentally, emotionally, and spiritually. On the other hand, self-worth is about recognizing your inherent value as a person, regardless of your relationship status.

Why do self-awareness and self-worth matter, especially after a divorce? Right now, everything around you feels uncertain, but by knowing yourself, you have an anchor that keeps you grounded. Understanding who you are and what you're worth will help you regain the confidence that may have been lost due to the divorce. Your worth isn't tied to your relationship status or any external validation—it's tied to who you are as a person. It can be measured by the kindness you show to others, the resilience you demonstrate in difficult times, the passions that drive you, and the values that guide your decisions. Recognizing these aspects of yourself can help rebuild confidence and provide a strong foundation for your future.

How Divorce Can Impact Self-Worth

In today's society, success in relationships is often portrayed as permanent. According to my parents, "Forever is the goal." When that didn't happen, I internalized a sense of failure, wondering, "What's wrong with me? Why couldn't I make it work?" These thoughts, while expected, can be incredibly damaging. They reduce the complexity of relationships to a black-and-white narrative of success and failure.

Society often adds to this pressure. While divorce is more accepted today, there's still an unspoken expectation to "bounce back" quickly. Well-meaning friends may say things like, "Don't worry, you'll find someone else soon," or "It's enough; just move on." Though meant to comfort, these comments can make it even harder to process emotions, implying that healing should have a timeline or that one's worth is tied to how fast they recover.

I had a colleague who shared his experience with me. After his divorce, his friends kept pushing him to re-enter the dating scene, recommending apps and telling him it would help him move on. But he wasn't ready—he needed time to reflect, grieve, and understand himself outside of being in a relationship. The pressure to "bounce back" only made him feel like he was failing again and nowhere near healing.

Divorce can create a deep sense of self-doubt, making you question whether you were a good partner, whether you are lovable, or whether you will ever find happiness again. These thoughts can seep into other areas of life, affecting relationships, confidence at work, and the ability to pursue personal goals. But self-worth isn't defined by a failed marriage—it's defined by who you are beyond it.

Rebuilding Your Self-Worth Post-Divorce

Rebuilding self-worth after divorce is possible, but it won't happen overnight. Some days, you'll feel lighter, and other days, you'll feel overwhelmed. The goal is to take steady steps toward emotional healing. Here are a few ways to strengthen your self-worth:

Remind Yourself of Your Strengths and Talents

Right now, it's easy to forget what makes you valuable. Divorce can cloud your sense of identity. Self-reflection is crucial—grab a notebook and start listing your strengths, achievements, and qualities. Maybe you're a great parent, a skilled professional, or a loyal friend. Recognize and celebrate these aspects of yourself.

At one point, I felt I had lost everything. I was so focused on what went wrong in my marriage that I forgot the good in my life. Inspired by advice from Dale Carnegie, I began writing a list of my strengths and achievements. Every day, I read it to remind myself of who I was outside of my marriage. Over time, this practice became a source of motivation, helping me shift my focus from what I had lost to what I still had. It reinforced my self-confidence and reminded me that my identity was not solely defined by my past relationship.

You are whole. You have value, strengths, and purpose—don't let your divorce make you forget that.

Identify Negative Self-Talk and Challenge It

Sometimes, our worst enemy is our own mind, especially during tough times. Right now, it's common to have thoughts like, "I'm not good enough," "I failed myself and everyone," or "No one will ever love me again." These thoughts may feel real, but they are negative self-talk—distorted perceptions fueled by your emotions.

Next time you have such thoughts, challenge them. For example, if you're thinking, "I'll never find someone who loves me," pause and ask yourself, "Is this really true?" Dig deeper, and you'll realize that this thought isn't based on fact but on current emotions. You're still healing and haven't put yourself out there yet. True love takes time to rediscover.

A helpful exercise is to write these negative thoughts down and then counter them with a more balanced and empowering statement. For example, if you think, "I'm not good enough," reframe it as "I'm growing every day and becoming the best version of myself." This method doesn't suppress negative thoughts but transforms them into something constructive.

As you continue to reframe your thoughts, your brain will gradually shift its focus toward your strengths rather than the perceived flaws your inner critic highlights.

Practice Self-Compassion

When was the last time you gave yourself a break and refrained from being overly self-critical? Divorce is emotionally exhausting, and it's easy to dwell on regrets. However, being too hard on yourself only keeps you stuck and prevents you from moving forward. Practicing self-compassion can help you heal.

Imagine a close friend going through a divorce. How would you comfort them? You wouldn't tell them they failed or that they're unlovable. Instead, you'd say, "I know this is really hard, but you're doing your best, and you'll get through it." Now, turn that kindness inward.

When you have a bad day or feel overwhelmed by emotions, acknowledge your feelings without judgment. Tell yourself, "It's okay to feel this way. This is part of the healing process, and I'm allowed to take my time." Accepting your emotions instead of criticizing yourself for having them is a powerful way to foster self-compassion and healing.

Set Boundaries and Prioritize Yourself

Rebuilding your self-worth means evaluating your relationships and setting necessary boundaries. This might involve limiting contact with your ex (if needed), avoiding people who bring negativity, and saying no to things that don't serve your well-being.

After my divorce, I was overwhelmed by unsolicited advice from well-meaning family members. Their constant opinions made me doubt my decisions and question my self-worth. Eventually, I realized I had to set boundaries to maintain my peace. I politely but firmly let them know that I appreciated their concern but needed space to make my own choices.

Say yes to the things that uplift you and no to the things that don't. This can include reconnecting with old friends, exploring a new hobby, or simply spending time alone. For me, I found solace in hiking. Walking through nature, feeling the fresh air, and hearing nothing but my own footsteps gave me the clarity I needed. Whatever brings you joy, engage in it—it reinforces the idea that you matter and are worth the effort.

Be Open to Support

Many people see reaching out for help as a sign of weakness, especially men. However, even the strongest individuals need support; seeking help is a sign of courage, not weakness. Unfortunately, many believe that asking for support makes them seem incapable or dependent when, in reality, it demonstrates self-awareness and strength. Overcoming the misconception that you must endure hardship alone can be one of the most transformative steps in healing. True strength lies in recognizing when you need support and taking proactive steps to seek guidance, whether from friends, family, or professionals.

Healing often comes through connection. When you surround yourself with the right support system—such as close family, friends, or even a therapist—you gain valuable perspective and guidance. People who truly know and care about you can offer insight that helps make your healing process less isolating.

Joining support groups can also be incredibly helpful. These communities allow you to connect with others who have experienced similar struggles and understand what you're going through. Consider joining a local or online divorce support group or seeking guidance from a professional therapist. These resources can provide a safe space to process your emotions and gain clarity on your healing journey.

Focus on Growth, Not Perfection

Healing isn't about achieving perfection—it's about growth. You're human, and you're allowed to make mistakes, feel uncertain, and experience setbacks. The key is to keep moving forward, even if the progress is slow.

Stop focusing on what you've lost; look ahead to what you can create. I once met a woman who, after her divorce, felt completely lost. She had spent years defining herself through her marriage, and when it ended, she wasn't sure who she was anymore. Instead of dwelling on the past, she decided to revisit an old passion—painting. What started as a small hobby soon turned into a successful business. By focusing on what she could create rather than what she had lost, she not only rebuilt her confidence but also found fulfillment in ways she never imagined.

You, too, have the power to shape your future in ways that align with your passions and dreams. Who do you want to become? Have you put off dreams and goals? Now is the time to explore them, grow, and rediscover yourself.

The most important relationship you will ever have is the one with yourself—make it a strong and nurturing one.

Managing Anger, Sadness, and Other Emotions After Divorce

Divorce will shake you up and bring intense emotions like anger, frustration, confusion, and sadness. You'll likely experience one emotion more intensely than the others or even feel multiple emotions at once. This is normal. There is no right or wrong way to feel when mourning the loss of your marriage—having all these emotions is a natural part of the healing process.

Being angry, sad, and experiencing other intense emotions doesn't mean you're weak or out of control. Allow yourself to feel them fully because suppressing them will only delay the healing process and cause more damage. Permit yourself to feel it all without judgment. Suppressing emotions may seem like a way to cope, but in reality, allowing yourself to experience them fully is essential for long-term healing. Acknowledging and processing your emotions helps prevent them from manifesting in unhealthy ways, such as stress, resentment, or avoidance. By giving yourself permission to grieve, reflect, and express what you feel, you create space for growth and emotional resilience.

5 Strategies for Managing Anger

Anger is one of the most common intense emotions you'll feel after divorce. You're angry for many reasons, and this feeling can be overwhelming if not managed effectively. To take a critical step toward healing, it's important to learn how to address and channel your anger constructively.

1. Express Your Anger Constructively

Anger itself isn't inherently bad; it's a signal that something matters to you. However, anger becomes harmful when expressed recklessly. Instead of suppressing it or lashing out, it's best to express it constructively.

- **Talk about it.** Vent to a trusted friend or therapist to help release the emotional pressure you feel. When sharing your feelings, avoid spiraling into blame by saying things like, "They always..." Instead, try saying, "I feel hurt because..." This way, your venting is more about healing rather than dwelling on negativity.

- **Write about your feelings.** When your emotions feel too big to handle, journaling can be an effective tool. Many people find that writing down their thoughts provides clarity and a sense of relief, helping them organize emotions in a way that makes them easier to process. Research suggests that journaling can reduce stress, improve mood, and strengthen problem-solving skills, making it an invaluable tool for emotional healing.

- **Avoid venting on social media.** While it may feel like an outlet, airing grievances online can have long-term consequences. Instead of bashing your ex publicly, focus on private, productive ways to work through your anger.

2. Explore Cooling-Off Techniques

Anger can escalate quickly, leading to words or actions you might regret. Learning to cool off in the heat of the moment can prevent unnecessary conflict.

- **Practice deep breathing exercises.** Use the "4-4-4" technique: inhale for four seconds, hold for four seconds, and exhale for four seconds. This slows your heart rate and calms your nervous system, helping you think clearly.

- **Take a break.** When emotions run high, stepping away from a heated situation—whether for a few minutes or a few hours—can help you gain perspective. For example, if a conversation with your ex starts escalating, excusing yourself for a short walk can help prevent unnecessary conflict and allow you to approach the situation with a clearer mind.

- **Visualize a peaceful place.** When overwhelmed, imagine yourself in a calm setting, such as a beach or a quiet park. This technique can help balance your emotions and reduce tension.

3. Redirect Your Anger Into Positive Actions

Channel your anger into productive activities that promote your physical and emotional well-being:

- **Exercise.** Activities like running, walking, or boxing can help burn off the adrenaline anger creates while releasing endorphins that improve your mood.

- **Creative outlets.** Engage in writing, painting, playing music, or redecorating a room to channel your emotions constructively.

4. Reframe Your Perspective on Anger

Sometimes, anger stems from deeper emotions like pain or fear. Ask yourself: *What is my anger trying to tell me?* Are you hurt because you feel betrayed? Are you afraid of facing the future alone? Understanding the root of your anger allows you to approach it with more compassion.

Instead of replaying your ex's actions in your mind, try reframing the situation: *"This anger is showing me that I cared deeply and expected more, and that's okay. I can't change the past, but I can choose how I respond moving forward."* This mindset shift can turn anger from an unproductive emotion into a catalyst for growth.

5. Build an Anger-Management Toolbox

Since anger can be an ongoing process, it's essential to have strategies in place:

- **Use meditation apps like Calm and Headspace** to manage stress and anger.

- **Practice mindfulness techniques,** such as deep breathing or progressive muscle relaxation, to regulate emotions.

- **Engage in physical activities** like yoga or running to channel anger into positive energy.

Anger can highlight what's important to you—your needs, values, and boundaries. When addressed and channeled well, it can serve as a tool for self-discovery.

Dealing With Sadness and Grief

Sadness and grief are some of the most overwhelming emotions you'll experience after divorce. It may feel like you've lost not just your partner but also a piece of yourself. This sadness is a natural part of grieving, and avoiding it will only delay healing. Permit yourself to feel these emotions without shame.

- **Journaling can help.** Writing down your emotions, even if messy or raw, can bring clarity and reveal patterns in your healing process.

- **Therapy is valuable.** A therapist can help you process grief, manage emotions, and rebuild your life after divorce.

- **Don't isolate yourself.** Seek support from friends, family, or support groups. Talking about your experiences can ease feelings of loneliness and provide comfort during difficult moments.

Handling Fear, Anxiety, and Guilt

Divorce stirs up various emotions beyond anger and sadness, including fear, anxiety, and guilt. Knowing how to manage these emotions can help calm your mind.

- **Manage fear and anxiety.** When uncertainty about your future feels overwhelming, use grounding exercises like the 5-4-3-2-1 technique: identify five things you can see, four you can touch, three you can hear, two you can smell, and one you can taste. This technique brings you back to the present moment and helps you regain control when your thoughts spiral.

- **Release guilt and self-blame.** It's easy to blame yourself for the end of your marriage and the impact on your loved ones. However, guilt is a destructive emotion. Instead of dwelling on regrets, reflect on your role in the relationship, learn from past mistakes, and focus on personal growth rather than self-punishment.

Managing emotions after divorce isn't always easy. But by understanding your feelings, allowing yourself to process them, and using practical strategies to cope, you can begin to regain control over them.

If you slip while trying to manage your emotions, don't be hard on yourself. Emotional healing isn't linear, and setbacks are a normal part of the process. I remember a time when I thought I had moved past my anger, only to have it resurface unexpectedly during a conversation with my ex. Instead of feeling like I had failed, I reminded myself that healing takes time and that progress isn't about never stumbling—it's about continuing to move forward despite the challenges. You're doing the best you can.

How to Release Resentment and Move Forward

Holding onto resentment after divorce feels like carrying a weight that only drags you down. Right now, you may feel hurt or betrayed, but allowing resentment to linger will keep you stuck in the past, clouding your future. Yes, it can feel justified to hold onto anger, but ultimately, resentment punishes you more than your ex.

Resentment can take a toll on both your mental and physical well-being, leading to chronic stress, anxiety, and even health issues such as high blood pressure or poor sleep. The longer you hold onto it, the more it drains your energy, making it harder to move forward and embrace new opportunities for growth and happiness. Letting go of resentment will allow you to experience the emotional freedom and peace you deserve.

The Power of Forgiveness

In this situation, forgiveness is a tool for releasing resentment. It frees you from the grip of negative emotions that have been holding you back. When you forgive, you release the power that your ex's actions have over you, allowing you to reclaim your peace.

Forgiveness isn't easy, but it is an important step toward emotional healing. And forgiveness isn't just for your ex—it's for you. You need to reclaim your peace of mind and emotional energy. By forgiving, you're not excusing past actions or allowing anger to control you; you're setting yourself free.

Journaling as a Tool for Healing

Like other emotions, you can release resentment through writing. Many people have found that structured journaling or letter-writing exercises help them process emotions in a constructive way. Writing a letter to your ex (without sending it) or keeping a forgiveness journal can provide clarity, allowing you to articulate your feelings and gradually let go of the weight of resentment.

Letting your feelings out through writing allows you to process them without judgment or confrontation. Over time, your perspective will shift, guiding you toward forgiveness.

Writing has helped countless people reframe their experiences and see a path forward with more clarity and less bitterness.

Practicing Mindfulness to Let Go

With mindfulness, you can observe your thoughts and emotions without becoming overwhelmed by them. Staying mindful will help you break free from the cycle of resentment by helping you recognize when your mind starts to go down a negative path. A simple breathing exercise, such as inhaling for four seconds, holding for four seconds, and exhaling for four seconds, can help train your mind to let go of grudges and focus on your own healing.

Being present in the moment rather than dwelling on past pain allows you to shift your focus to what you can control. With consistent mindfulness practice, resentment will lose its grip on you, allowing you to live more freely and fully.

Seeking Support to Move Forward

Sometimes, holding onto resentment means you're not expressing your feelings to anyone who can truly understand. Seeking support from a therapist, a trusted friend, or a support group can provide a safe space to process your emotions. Talking to someone who has been through a similar experience can offer perspective, reassurance, and practical advice to help you let go of resentment and move forward.

Support groups and therapy can be powerful tools in healing. Hearing others' stories, sharing your own, and receiving guidance from professionals can help you reframe your emotions and see new possibilities for the future. You don't have to go through this alone—connection can be one of the strongest antidotes to resentment.

Embracing a Fresh Start

When you truly let go of resentment, you start to heal and feel a sense of empowerment by taking control of your emotions. Let go and shed the emotional baggage that keeps you trapped in the past. You'll start to feel lighter, become more open to opportunities, and gain the confidence to start a new chapter.

Now is the time to find hope, clarity, passions, dreams, and new relationships; embrace the possibility of a fresh start. I once knew someone who, after years of struggling with resentment, decided to channel their energy into a new hobby—photography. What started as a simple distraction turned into a passion that connected them with new friends, opened up creative opportunities, and ultimately helped them redefine their sense of purpose. Moving forward isn't about forgetting the past; it's about actively building a future that excites and fulfills you.

It's time to move forward! This doesn't mean forgetting the lessons you've learned or erasing your past. Instead, it means creating a future you'll be proud of—one that isn't defined by regret or resentment. Let go, embrace your emotional freedom, and step into a life of greater peace.

Chapter Key Points:

- Emotional resilience is your inner strength to face challenges, helping you bounce back stronger after setbacks.

- Adversity is inevitable, but how you respond to it defines your growth. Resilience is built by accepting change, reframing negativity, and focusing on what you can control.

- Be kind to yourself during tough times to prevent burnout and truly heal from your divorce.

- Starting a new chapter isn't a one-time achievement. It requires practice, patience, and a supportive network.

- Embrace your journey, reclaim your inner power, and see life's challenges as opportunities for personal growth.

Chapter Three

Redefining Your Life:

Personal Growth After Divorce

"The best way to predict the future is to create it."
- Abraham Lincoln

Are You Moving Toward Your Goals?

Are you any closer to your goals, or do they seem far from reach? Do you still know who you want to become? What about what you stand for?

You might see these questions as rhetorical or irrelevant to your life right now. But don't shrug them off, hoping they'll resolve themselves. These answers hold the key to rediscovering yourself and building a life where you're not just surviving but thriving. Even after divorce, you have the power to redefine your future.

Embracing a New Beginning

Divorce can turn your life upside down, forcing you to confront aspects of yourself that you may have ignored for years—your personal goals, friendships, and self-care. Maybe you put your career aspirations on hold to support your spouse, drifted away from hobbies you once loved, or lost touch with close friends. Now, you have an opportunity to reexamine these areas and reclaim what truly matters to you. While it can feel disorienting and even terrifying, this is your chance to rebuild your life from the ground up.

I'm not suggesting that you need to be divorced to redefine your life and be better. What I'm saying is that now is the time to pick yourself up and get back on track.

Rediscovering Your Identity

To get this right, start with yourself. Do you know your strengths and weaknesses? Be completely honest—there's no need to impress anyone or sugarcoat your flaws. This life you're building is for you, not for others. Understanding the raw materials you're working with will help you shape yourself into something great.

For many years, your identity might have shifted due to your marriage as you took on roles and responsibilities that defined your daily life. Perhaps you prioritized being a spouse and parent over personal ambitions, adjusted your interests to align with your partner's, or lost touch with what once made you feel uniquely you. Now, you have the opportunity to rediscover yourself—whether that means rekindling an old passion, pursuing a new career path, or redefining your values and goals on your own terms.

If you once had big dreams but set them aside, now is the time to revisit them. Reflect on what once excited you and take concrete steps toward making those dreams a reality. Whether it's climbing the corporate ladder, starting a new business, or picking up a long-lost hobby, every step you take brings you closer to your future goals. You need to turn your vision into a plan and map out small steps that will take you closer to your desired future.

Setting Boundaries and Reclaiming Your Time

Divorce teaches an important lesson—the value of drawing boundaries and sticking to them. Not out of spite, but out of self-respect. Who truly deserves your time, energy, and attention? Your time is now a precious resource; learn to use it wisely.

This chapter focuses on redefining your life. We won't pretend that your experience didn't hurt or try to erase the past. Instead, we'll take the pieces of your old life and rearrange them into something more intentional, stronger, and entirely your own. Get ready to reclaim control and create a life with purpose and identity.

Identifying Core Strengths and Weaknesses

I've been there—standing at a crossroads, feeling lost, and questioning my identity outside of my marriage. When my life shifted so drastically, it was natural to focus on what I had lost. Looking back, I wish I had paid more attention to Sun Tzu's words in *The Art of War*: "In the midst of chaos, there is also opportunity."

Had I embraced that wisdom earlier, I might have saved myself years of suffering before finding my footing and setting things right. Instead of understanding who I was so I could build a future I was proud of, I spent years labeling myself by my past.

Be Self-Aware

The way forward starts by looking inward. If you're like my old self—unsure of your next step—pause and reflect. Ask yourself:

- What are my greatest strengths?

- What challenges have I overcome?

- What do those victories say about me?

- What areas of my life feel like stumbling blocks, and how can I turn them into stepping stones?

This process requires courage, but it's essential for growth. Studies show that self-reflection helps people manage stress, build stronger relationships, and achieve their goals. By understanding your emotions, values, and unique strengths, you lay the groundwork for personal growth and better decision-making.

Positive psychology emphasizes this concept, stating that when you focus on your strengths and abilities, you build resilience. You become better equipped to face challenges with confidence and optimism, ultimately enhancing your overall life satisfaction.

Turning Weaknesses into Strengths

Self-awareness isn't just about recognizing strengths; it's also about acknowledging weaknesses and using them as opportunities for growth.

1. **Identify Your Strengths** – List your accomplishments, both big and small. Recognize moments when you demonstrated resilience, courage, or kindness.

2. **Acknowledge Your Weaknesses** – Don't view them as failures; instead, see them as areas for improvement. For example, if setting boundaries is difficult for you, start practicing small ways to assert yourself.

3. **Create a Strengths and Weaknesses Table** – Write down your strengths, weaknesses, and actionable steps to improve.

Rebuilding Your Social Circle

One of the biggest challenges after divorce is rebuilding your social life. Right now, meeting new people might feel intimidating—but don't rush it. Start with small, manageable steps:

- Reconnect with old friends.

- Join a group or class that interests you.

- Attend local events or community gatherings.

I remember feeling isolated after my divorce until I decided to join a gym. At first, it was just about staying active, but over time, I built friendships and found a sense of fulfillment I hadn't felt in years. Small steps like these can make a big difference.

Moving Forward With Confidence

Each step you take toward addressing your weaknesses strengthens your sense of self. By seeing your strengths, weaknesses, and everything in between, you're laying the foundation for a fulfilling and empowered future.

Yes, you might still feel knocked down after your divorce, but don't let it define you. Taking time to reflect on who you are will give you the tools to move forward with confidence and clarity. You are not starting over—you're building something new, and this time, it's entirely yours.

Embracing Transformation

Creating a vision for your future means rediscovering who you are, embracing new possibilities, and building a life that reflects your passions, values, and dreams.

Every ending holds the potential for a transformative beginning. While closing one chapter can be painful, it also creates space for reinvention and new opportunities. Divorce, while challenging, offers a unique chance to reshape your life in ways that align with your deepest aspirations and values.

Envisioning Your Ideal Life

What does your ideal life look like without limitations? For many, the demands of marriage, parenting, and daily responsibilities push personal dreams aside. After divorce, those dreams might feel buried under the weight of loss and uncertainty. But this is your chance to unearth them and start anew.

Now is the time to envision the life you truly want to live. Use this moment as a fresh start to create a future that reflects who you are now and who you want to become.

1. Clarify Your Vision

The first step in creating a vision for your future is gaining clarity. It's difficult to build a fulfilling life if you're unsure of what you want. Take time to reflect, dream, and set meaningful goals.

Reflect on Your Passions

What excites you? What makes you feel alive?

For years, you may have prioritized your partner, children, and career. While these are essential, it's equally important to remember the hobbies and activities that once brought you joy.

For instance, I've always loved writing, but during my marriage, I never made time for it. After my divorce, I rediscovered my passion for it. Writing became both a source of joy and a way to process my emotions. For you, it might be something entirely different—starting a business, painting, gardening, or even cooking. Whatever it is, reconnecting with your passions can help you rebuild your identity.

Visualize Your Future

Many people think visualization is just daydreaming, but it's more than that. Visualization is a scientifically backed method that helps focus your mind on what you want to achieve. By vividly imagining your desired outcome, you can boost motivation and improve your chances of success.

To visualize your future, start by creating a vision board. I once met a woman who, after her divorce, felt lost and uncertain. She created a vision board filled with images of places she wanted to visit, career aspirations, and qualities she wanted to develop. Seeing those goals daily motivated her to take small steps toward achieving them. Within a year, she had traveled to two dream destinations and launched the business she had always wanted. A vision board serves as a constant reminder of what's possible and inspires you to take action.

Another powerful technique is writing a letter to your future self. Describe your dream life in detail—where you live, what your daily routine looks like, and how you feel when you wake up each morning. Putting these thoughts into words solidifies them in your mind and turns them into actionable goals.

Set Achievable Goals

Big dreams can feel overwhelming. That's why it's essential to break them into smaller, more manageable steps.

- **Career Goals:** If you've always dreamed of switching careers, start by researching industries that fascinate you or enrolling in online courses to build new skills.

- **Adventure Goals:** If traveling excites you, plan a weekend getaway first and create a savings plan for a bigger trip.

- **Relationship Goals:** If you seek deeper connections with loved ones, start by sending handwritten notes, committing to regular dinner dates, or having heartfelt conversations.

Even small goals can have a meaningful impact. What matters is taking intentional steps toward your ideal future.

2. Encourage Growth

True transformation involves growth in all areas of your life—mental, physical, and emotional. Each area is interconnected, and progress in one fuels growth in another.

Mental Growth

Your divorce may have challenged your sense of identity, but it has also opened the door to self-discovery. The mental strength that has helped you survive can be channeled into achieving your goals. Learn a new skill, join a group that expands your perspective, or start a journal to track your progress.

Physical Growth

Taking care of your body is just as important as nurturing your mind. Prioritize nutrition, exercise, and self-care to feel strong, capable, and energized. Start small—take a daily walk, establish a restful bedtime routine, or try a new healthy recipe.

Emotional Growth

Emotional healing is crucial for moving forward. Start by practicing self-compassion—acknowledge your feelings without judgment and speak to yourself with kindness. Engage in activities that make you feel good, whether it's journaling, meditation, or spending time on hobbies. Strengthening relationships involves setting healthy boundaries, expressing gratitude, and being present with those who matter. Prioritize connections with people who uplift and support you, and don't be afraid to seek professional help if needed.

When you focus on growth in these areas, you create a strong foundation for lasting change.

3. Overcome the Fear of the Unknown

Dreaming big can be scary. The fear of failure, uncertainty, or stepping outside your comfort zone can feel overwhelming. However, these fears often stem from past experiences or limiting beliefs. Instead of seeing them as obstacles, reframe them as signs that you're pushing yourself toward growth and new possibilities.

The future is uncertain, and stepping outside your comfort zone often brings fear and self-doubt. But the truth is that growth and comfort don't go hand in hand. To create a life you love, you must embrace a little discomfort.

When fear or doubt creeps in, remind yourself of the strengths you've identified. Use them as anchors to guide you through uncertainty. If resilience is one of your strengths, reflect on past challenges you've overcome. If creativity is your strength, channel it into finding solutions to obstacles that arise.

4. Strengthen Relationships and Social Circles

If you have children, include them in your vision for the future. Think about how your goals can provide stability and fulfillment for them. What kind of parent do you want to be? Strengthen bonds by engaging in open conversations, spending regular one-on-one time, or creating new family traditions.

If you've lost touch with friends or family members, start reconnecting. Reach out and let them know how you feel. Relationships are an essential part of a fulfilling life—nurture them.

One of the biggest challenges after divorce is rebuilding your social life. Meeting new people might feel intimidating, but start small:

- Reconnect with old friends.

- Join a class or group aligned with your interests.

- Attend local events or community gatherings.

After my divorce, I joined a gym. Initially, it was just about staying active, but over time, I built friendships and found a renewed sense of fulfillment. Small steps like these can make a big difference in rebuilding your social network.

Moving Forward With Confidence

Creating a vision for yourself should be taken one step at a time. Progress may feel slow, but every small effort brings you closer to the future you desire. Trust the process, celebrate your wins along the way, and embrace the journey of growth and transformation.

You won't have everything figured out immediately. Start small and build from there. Each step, no matter how small, is progress. Take your time with this process—your future is yours to shape.

Defining Your Boundaries

You've created a vision for your future—what's next? It's time to reset the rules. You need to take stock, reflect, and redefine how you engage with the world. This starts with setting boundaries.

Before we get to that, I need to make something clear. Setting boundaries isn't just about shutting certain people out or building walls; it's about fostering healthier relationships and protecting your well-being. Boundaries help you create space for meaningful connections while ensuring that your needs and values are respected. More importantly, they establish a healthier and more intentional relationship with yourself. Boundaries are your way of saying, "This is what I need to thrive, and I won't compromise on it."

But why are boundaries crucial, especially now that you're starting a new chapter? Boundaries protect your energy, nurture your well-being, and set the tone for healthy interactions. After divorce, emotions can be overwhelming, and expectations may feel heavy; boundaries become a powerful tool to reclaim control, rebuild confidence, and restore self-worth.

How Boundaries Empower You

When you set boundaries, you start living intentionally instead of reactively. You take control of how you spend your time, energy, and emotional resources rather than being at the mercy of others' expectations.

Over time, your self-respect, confidence, and resilience will strengthen. You'll attract people and opportunities that align with your values. Your relationships will become more authentic, and your goals will feel more meaningful.

As a newly divorced man, I was constantly overextending myself to please others. I would say yes to everyone's requests—running errands for friends, covering for co-workers, and even staying up late to help others complete their tasks. The constant need to be available drained me physically and emotionally, leaving little time for my own healing and growth.

Setting boundaries wasn't easy for me. When I started, I felt guilty, and people were surprised because I had always been the "Mr. Nice Guy" who never said no. But as I continued saying no to unnecessary demands and stepping away from my people-pleasing habits, I started having more time for what mattered. I spent more time with my kids and pursued dreams I had once neglected.

Steps to Set Healthy Boundaries

Ready to set boundaries? Follow these steps to ensure you're protecting your well-being while staying true to your values.

1. Know Your Limits

First, recognize that your boundaries should be non-negotiable. What typically drains your energy or makes you feel undervalued? Think about your physical, mental, and emotional needs in different areas of your life, including work, relationships, and social settings.

For example, your limits might include setting specific work hours to ensure personal or family time, refusing to tolerate disrespectful behavior, and saying no to commitments that don't align with your values. Identifying your limits provides clarity on where boundaries are most needed.

2. Communicate Clearly

Your boundaries will only work when you communicate them effectively. I once assumed that people would naturally understand my limits without me having to say anything, but this led to misunderstandings and frustration. For instance, a friend would repeatedly call me late at night to vent, assuming I was always available. When I finally expressed that I needed to prioritize my rest and personal time, they were initially taken aback, but over time, they adjusted and respected my space. Clear communication eliminates confusion and ensures that your boundaries are acknowledged and respected.

Don't expect people to know what you want—speak with clarity, respect, and confidence without apologizing or feeling guilty. You could say, "I need to leave work by 6 p.m. to attend to personal commitments," or "I'm not comfortable discussing this topic. Let's talk about something else."

You aren't responsible for how others react to your boundaries. If someone responds negatively, it reflects their perspective, not your worth.

3. Enforce Your Boundaries

You've done the easier part—setting boundaries. Now, it's time to enforce them! This requires courage and consistency. When someone crosses a boundary, address it calmly but firmly. For example, you could say, "I've mentioned that I have personal commitments to attend to. Please respect that moving forward."

At first, it'll feel uncomfortable because you aren't used to turning people down. It took me months before setting boundaries felt natural. Initially, I struggled with guilt and second-guessed myself, but over time, I realized that prioritizing my well-being was necessary. The discomfort eventually faded as I saw the positive changes in my life, making it easier to stand firm in my decisions.

You may have been a people-pleaser or a conflict-avoider for a long time, but enforcing boundaries is essential. Each time you stand firm, you reinforce your self-respect and strengthen your commitment to your well-being.

4. Elevate Your Personal Standards

While boundaries define how others treat you, your standards determine how you treat yourself. The two go hand in hand. Now, you have the opportunity to raise your standards if you haven't already. Elevating your personal standards sets the bar for the life you deserve.

This could mean prioritizing your physical and mental health as non-negotiable, refusing to tolerate toxic behaviors, or setting ambitious goals without settling for less. Your standards should reflect the kind of life you truly want to create.

As you strive for a life that aligns with your dreams and values, be kind to yourself. Perfection isn't the goal—progress is. Each step toward higher standards builds the foundation for the fulfilling life you envision.

By setting boundaries, elevating your standards, and committing to your growth, you are building a strong foundation for a fulfilling future. Every decision you make to protect your energy and prioritize your well-being is a step toward the life you deserve. Keep pushing forward, stay true to your values, and embrace the journey of transformation—your best days are ahead. Your growth is important, and every step taken and standard set counts. Stay with me as we discuss rebuilding your relationships in the next chapter.

Chapter Key Points

- Knowing your strengths and weaknesses gives you clarity and direction for personal growth.

- Divorce is a fresh start; it offers you the chance to rediscover your passions and create a life that aligns with your values.

- Use visual tools like vision boards and goal-setting to stay focused on building the future you want.

- Setting and enforcing clear boundaries ensures you prioritize your needs.

- Personal growth after divorce requires patience, self-awareness, and consistent effort.

- Each small step you take to rebuild your life is essential in redefining yourself and moving toward a fulfilling future.

Chapter Four

Rebuilding Relationships:

Friends, Family, and New Connections

"The only way to have a friend is to be one."
- Ralph Waldo Emerson

The Silence After Separation

The moment my divorce was finalized, I felt an unexpected and crushing silence in my life. I had assumed my support system would remain unchanged, but instead, I found myself facing an emptiness I hadn't anticipated. I received little to no invitations from my social circle. The mutual friends I shared with my ex were quietly fading away, and my family was treading on eggshells whenever they were with me. I had once relished the social calendar I maintained as part of a couple, but after the divorce, my evenings were spent in a quiet apartment with stings of loneliness.

For months, I lay on my couch, wondering if this was my new normal. I questioned where I fit in without the identity of someone's partner and whether I could truly connect with others again.

One day, after yet another evening spent alone with my thoughts, fueled by boredom and desperation, I picked up my phone and scrolled through my contacts. The weight of my solitude had finally pushed me to seek connection, even if it meant reaching out to someone I hadn't spoken to in years. For the first time in years, I realized how many names belonged to people I hadn't spoken to in months or even years.

Reaching Out: A Leap of Faith

One name that stood out was Dave. He was my close friend in high school, someone who knew all my quirks, dreams, and bad decisions. Over time, our lives drifted apart. We stopped checking in as often, and before I knew it, months turned into years without a real conversation. We both got busy with careers, relationships, and the everyday demands of adulthood, and our once-frequent conversations became rare. Still, I couldn't shake the feeling that reaching out to him might be worth it. I debated texting him for hours, my finger hovering over his name, before finally typing, "Hi, Dave. It's been way too long. I'd love to catch up. Are you free to grab a drink?"

After a couple of hours, I checked my phone and saw no response. "Maybe he didn't want to talk to me or no longer uses this number," I thought. The next morning, I woke up to an enthusiastic response from Dave. He was happy to hear from me and couldn't wait to meet up.

That one text turned into a coffee date that gave me hours of laughter. I rekindled a friendship I hadn't realized I missed so much. Slowly, I started rebuilding relationships and began to feel like myself again.

The Ripple Effect of Divorce on Relationships

As I navigated my own shifting relationships, I realized that divorce doesn't just affect the couple—it reshapes social circles in unexpected ways. Your divorce has probably reshaped your relationship with your now-former partner and your connections with others. Perhaps some friends who were close to both you and your ex now feel uncertain about how to fit into your lives.

On the other hand, family members might overreact by either giving you uncomfortable distance or smothering concern. This leaves you with broken relationships around you, with mutual friends drifting or taking sides.

You're writing a new chapter for yourself, but the thought of rebuilding your relationships, whether platonic or romantic, feels overwhelming. Relationships are important; no one should be an island. Moreover, relationships are not just about companionship or filling a void—they bring happiness, growth, and even healing.

Reconnecting with Old Friends

Divorce can be an isolating experience. You lost a partner and also the community that came with the relationship. Now that you're rewriting your chapter, it's time to rediscover friendships you may have neglected or overlooked for too long.

My experience with Mark taught me that old friendships, even those seemingly lost to time, could be revived with a little courage and effort.

Research suggests that reconnecting with old friends can improve one's emotional well-being. Ever heard that familiarity breeds comfort? Reconnecting with people who have known you for a long time can provide the support you need to restore your sense of identity. A report by the American Psychological Association (APA) revealed that social connections are directly linked to better mental and physical health outcomes.

Steps to Reconnect With Old Friends

Rebuilding old friendships after divorce can be intimidating. It's natural to feel hesitant because these are people you haven't reached out to in a long time, and you may be unsure of how to go about it or where to start. The following steps can make reconnection less intimidating and more successful.

1. Be Honest When Reaching Out

The first step is usually the hardest. Since it's been a long time since you last connected, you may worry about the other person's reaction. When reaching out, start with a heartfelt message that shows warmth and honesty. For example, "I know it's been a while, but I've been thinking about you and would love to reconnect," or "Hi, I miss our talks. Would you be open to catching up soon?"

This type of message is low-pressure but conveys your genuine desire to reconnect. Keep it straightforward and focus on your intent rather than overthinking how the other person might react.

Besides Dave, I also reached out to an old college friend, Ann. At first, I was nervous because we hadn't spoken in nearly five years, and I wasn't sure if she would want to talk to me at all. I summoned the courage to send a message: "Hey Ann, I just wanted to let you know that I've been thinking about you. Life hasn't been a pleasure cruise, and I've missed you. Would you like to grab a coffee sometime?" Surprisingly, her response was positive.

Sometimes, people are just waiting for someone to make the first move; bridge that gap by taking the initiative.

2. Don't Rush It; Start Slow

It can feel awkward to reach out to someone after a long time, especially after a disagreement or when your lives have taken different paths. Taking it slow and starting small can make a difference.

Don't expect the relationship to pick up exactly where it left off. People change over time, and some friendships may no longer fit into your life the way they once did. It's okay if a connection doesn't rekindle as expected—what matters is that you made the effort, and sometimes, letting go is just as valuable as holding on. For example, a friend who was once spontaneous and carefree might now have a structured routine due to family or work commitments. Understanding and embracing these changes can help ease the transition into a renewed connection.

Start by suggesting a casual reconnection, such as a coffee meet-up at a cozy café, going for a walk in a park, or scheduling a brief phone or video call to ease into catching up.

When I reconnected with Mark, I suggested meeting at a coffee shop we both loved back in the day. The place brought back shared memories and allowed us to ease into deeper conversations naturally.

3. It's Okay To Be Vulnerable

True friendships allow you to be yourself. Embracing vulnerability fosters deeper trust by demonstrating honesty and emotional maturity. When you openly share your fears, hopes, and struggles, it invites reciprocity and reassures your friend that they can do the same, ultimately strengthening the bond between you. While it's okay to keep conversations surface-level to avoid discomfort, sharing your true emotions without masking them helps rebuild trust and deepen your connection.

Vulnerability shows trust and emotional maturity. It encourages reciprocity, where your friend may feel comfortable sharing their own struggles, laying a foundation for a more meaningful relationship moving forward.

At first, I was hesitant to open up when I met Mark. But after a few meetings, I decided to be honest about why I reached out. I told him, "I've been feeling a little lost since the divorce, and I realized how much I missed having you in my life." His response was warm and understanding: "I've missed you too, and I'm always here for you."

Society has often discouraged men from showing vulnerability. Initially, it was difficult for me to express my emotions. However, I am glad I shared that vulnerability with my friend because it created an emotional bridge that rekindled our friendship.

Overcoming Common Challenges with Reconnection

Even with the best intentions, reconnecting with old friends isn't always smooth sailing. Challenges may arise that deter the intent. Below are common challenges you might face and ways to overcome them:

Unmet Expectations

It's natural to hope that an old friendship will return to how it was before. But that might not always be the case. When your expectation of getting your friendship back on track doesn't work out, don't be hard on yourself. Remember that people change over time, and so do relationships.

To manage your expectations, be open to the possibility that your connection may look different now. Take time to reflect on why you want to reconnect and what you hope to gain from the relationship. Instead of focusing on restoring the past, embrace the chance to create a new dynamic based on who you both are today. If feelings of disappointment arise, acknowledge them, but remind yourself that change is natural. A practical approach is to set small, realistic expectations—perhaps start with casual conversations before assuming a deeper bond will automatically return. Some friendships may not rekindle, and that's okay. Cherish the positive memories without dwelling on what could have been.

Awkwardness

The initial meeting or conversation with an old friend can sometimes feel awkward, especially if you've both been out of touch for a long time.

To ease the awkwardness, think about the memories you shared. This can create a sense of familiarity. Ask open-ended questions about their life, such as, "What's been keeping you busy these days?" If appropriate, lighten the mood with humor to make the conversation more comfortable.

Fear of Rejection

Reaching out can feel intimidating, especially if the friendship ended on a sour note or has been dormant for years. Before doing so, take some time to reflect on the nature of your past relationship and whether reconnecting would be beneficial for both of you. Consider factors such as how the friendship ended, whether unresolved conflicts exist, and whether you both have grown in ways that would support a positive reconnection. If you're unsure, start with a simple message to gauge their openness before investing emotionally. However, some people are more forgiving and open than we often assume, so don't let the fear of rejection stop you from trying.

According to psychologist Brené Brown, vulnerability is a strength, not a weakness. Take the risk to reconnect, even if the response isn't what you hoped for.

In fact, I experienced this firsthand with Mark when I didn't get an immediate response from him. Initially, I felt hurt, but then I reminded myself that he might be busy or dealing with his own challenges. We hadn't spoken in nearly five years, partly due to a minor argument we never resolved. I eventually reached out, knowing that even if he rejected my attempt, I'd feel proud of myself for trying.

Despite replying to my text the next day, when we met, he apologized for the late response, explaining that he had been overwhelmed with work. He also admitted that he had missed our friendship but didn't know how to approach me.

By understanding these challenges and using the strategies discussed, you can rekindle meaningful connections.

Make Peace with Your Past

Making peace with your past entails addressing unresolved emotions. If your relationship ended awkwardly or there's lingering tension, it's time to acknowledge and discuss it. Explain yourself and apologize when necessary. This is essential for your healing and a fresh start.

For example, when I reached out to Mark and we met, I made it a point to address our past misunderstanding by saying, "I've thought about what happened between us a lot, and I regret how I handled it. I'm sorry if I hurt you." Though this apology was simple and short, it opened the door for Mark to share his perspective, and we were able to move forward without resentment.

Don't forget to celebrate the people who have shaped you and stood by you during difficult times. Small gestures, such as sending a thoughtful message, remembering birthdays, or simply checking in, can strengthen these bonds and make them feel valued.

Reconnecting with old friends is a courageous step toward healing. The process may be slow, and not every attempt will lead to the outcome you hope for, but making an effort is something to be proud of.

Navigating Family Dynamics Post-Divorce

Even though you are the one who got divorced, the end of your marriage affects not just you but everyone connected to you. Your children, parents, siblings, extended family members, and friends may experience their own emotional fallout, including confusion and sadness. Dynamics shift, roles change, and sometimes, unspoken tensions surface, affecting how family members interact daily. Conversations may become strained, certain topics might feel off-limits, and moments that once felt natural can turn awkward. Adjusting to these new interactions requires patience and open communication to rebuild a sense of normalcy.

When I went through my divorce, my parents were devastated. My mom, in particular, wanted every detail of it. She constantly talked to me about the divorce, offered advice I didn't ask for, and even tried to mediate—unintentionally amplifying the tension. On the other hand, my dad grew distant. This wasn't the future he had envisioned for his children, and he struggled to address the situation.

One important thing to remember when navigating family dynamics is that your family members won't always know how to handle your pain—or even their own. Some may try to fix things to make you happy, while others might take sides or withdraw altogether. This can make you feel isolated.

Research suggests that extended relatives, especially those with close ties to your ex, may distance themselves, while immediate family members might attempt to overcompensate by becoming more involved in your life. These shifting dynamics can create emotional strain, requiring careful navigation to maintain balance and well-being. Navigating these changes can be challenging, but strengthening meaningful relationships and setting boundaries that protect your peace is essential.

Managing family dynamics might not please everyone or meet their expectations. However, prioritizing self-care and emotional well-being is crucial—healing and stability take precedence over meeting others' expectations. Be patient, set boundaries, rebuild connections, and calmly address criticism to ensure you have relationships that nurture your well-being.

Strategies for Navigating Family Dynamics

Perhaps your family members hold different biases, emotions, and opinions about your divorce, making an already difficult experience even more complex. Using thoughtful strategies and clear communication can help establish healthier dynamics that prioritize your well-being.

1. Set Boundaries

In the last chapter, we discussed setting boundaries to redefine one's life. Here, we can't overemphasize the importance of setting boundaries to navigate family dynamics. Some family members undoubtedly mean well, but their countless questions, unsolicited advice, and attempts to intervene in what has already ended can feel overwhelming and intrusive. Establishing boundaries is essential to protecting your mental and emotional health.

Why do boundaries matter? They define what's acceptable for you and what's not during this vulnerable period. Clear boundaries create space for healing and minimize unnecessary stress.

When my mother repeatedly brought up my ex during family dinners, I had to have a candid conversation with her and respectfully set things straight. I said, "Mom, I know you're worried about me, but bringing up my ex makes it harder for me to move forward. Can we please focus on the present instead?" Though it wasn't an easy conversation, it helped her understand my perspective and gave me the space I needed to process my emotions.

When setting boundaries, be polite but firm. Use "I" statements to express your feelings without blaming others. For example, you can say, "I appreciate your concern, but talking about my ex isn't helpful for me right now." Or, "I know you're trying to help by playing mediator, but I need to handle this in my own way."

Reinforce your boundaries when they are crossed by reminding the person of your needs. If someone continues to violate your boundaries, take a step back or temporarily limit interactions.

2. Focus on Supportive Relationships

Not all family members will provide the support you need during a challenging time like a divorce. While some readily offer genuine love and encouragement, others may add to your stress with more drama and judgment—though this may be unintentional.

Identify those who consistently uplift and encourage you. They are the ones who provide a safe space for emotional healing, offering words of encouragement and a listening ear without judgment. For example, a close friend who checks in on you regularly or a sibling who shares uplifting advice can make a significant difference in your recovery process. These are the people you should lean on during tough times.

Your support system can include a sibling, cousin, family friend, therapist, or support group. Seeking professional or community-based support can be just as valuable in providing guidance and reassurance during challenging times. I was surprised to find solace in my cousin. She had been through a divorce years earlier and understood my experience. Her empathy and wisdom were invaluable when other relatives seemed more interested in sharing their opinions than offering support.

Prioritize relationships with those who bring you peace and support. If certain people are critical or unsupportive, it's okay to create some distance. Preserve your energy for relationships that truly matter. Share your feelings openly and spend quality time with those who bring you comfort—whether it's taking a walk, eating out, or simply chatting.

Don't forget to express your gratitude for their support. A heartfelt thank-you, a thoughtful note, or a kind gesture can reinforce the positive aspects of your relationship and strengthen your bond over time.

3. Be Patient

As you adjust to your new life after divorce, your family members are also experiencing shifts in dynamics. Your divorce might have affected how they view and interact with you and your ex, especially when children are involved. They may need time to process their own emotions.

Understand their perspective, knowing that they have their emotional struggles. For example, your parents may feel guilt or sadness if they had a close bond with your ex.

Your siblings might struggle to cope with divided loyalties, and extended relatives could be unsure how to support you. Acknowledge these struggles and approach conversations with compassion.

When my father seemed distant after my divorce, I initially felt hurt. Later, I realized he was struggling to come to terms with his own feelings of loss. I decided to have an open conversation with him one day.

I told him, "Dad, I know this might've been hard on you too. I want you to know that I appreciate your support, even if we don't talk about it much." He responded by reassuring me of his love and concern, even if he expressed them differently than I had expected.

Allow time for your family to adjust to the new normal, just as you need grace for this phase. Don't take reactions personally; instead, encourage open communication. Let them know you're open to discussing their feelings when they're ready.

4. Dealing with Judgment or Criticism

From a place of concern or love, your family members may express disappointment, judgment, or unsolicited advice about your divorce using words that sting. But this shouldn't make you react rashly.

When this happens, don't react defensively. Take a deep breath and remain calm. Redirect the conversation to focus on the positive aspects of your journey. For example, you can say, "I understand that my divorce may not align with your expectations, but I'm doing what's best for my well-being." Or, "I appreciate your perspective, but I'd rather focus on how I'm moving forward."

Sometimes, criticism stems from other people's fears or insecurities. When my cousin expressed disappointment about my divorce, I reminded myself that her comments reflected her own beliefs about marriage rather than my situation. I didn't allow her words to bring me down; instead, I chose to focus on the support I was receiving from others who truly understood my journey.

Studies show that family support plays a critical role in recovery after divorce. People with strong family support can experience lower levels of depression, anxiety, and stress post-divorce. However, the quality of that support is more important than the quantity.

A supportive network provides empathy, understanding, and encouragement without judgment or unsolicited advice.

On the other hand, toxic dynamics that encourage criticism, over-involvement, or pressure can hinder healing and lead to feelings of inadequacy. For instance, if a relative constantly questions your decision to divorce or pressures you to reconcile, it can create unnecessary stress and self-doubt. To address this, set clear boundaries by saying something like, "I appreciate your concern, but I need to make decisions that align with my well-being." Redirect conversations when they become intrusive and focus on relationships that support your healing process. This is why it is crucial to set boundaries and prioritize healthy relationships.

5. Rebuilding Trust and Understanding

After a divorce, it's easy for family dynamics to be strained or broken, especially when your choices conflict with your family's hopes, values, and expectations. This is a challenging moment, but it can also be an opportunity to rebuild trust.

During my divorce, my relationship with my mom became tense. Due to our family values, she couldn't comprehend why my marriage ended, and she was always quick to voice her disappointment. I saw her attempts to fix the situation by pressuring me to reconcile with my ex as intrusive and dismissive of my emotions.

One day, I snapped and told her outright that I didn't want her involvement, especially now that the marriage had ended. It was painful to do that because I knew she was trying to look out for me, but boundaries needed to be set. That moment left us both hurt and emotionally distant. For weeks, we barely spoke, and when we saw each other, our eyes were filled with tension and unspoken pain.

After weeks of strained silence and emotional distance, I eventually realized that avoiding my mom wouldn't mend our relationship. I decided to have a conversation with her, pouring out my thoughts and feelings. I explained the personal challenges I was facing, the reasons behind my decision to divorce, and how much I valued her presence in my life, even if we didn't agree on everything.

She responded calmly, sharing her fears and worries for my future, which helped me understand her perspective better. This acknowledgment opened the door for a more honest dialogue, allowing us to rebuild trust and strengthen our relationship. She also acknowledged her missteps and expressed her desire to always support me. I was glad I had the conversation with her. With such honest communication, we could rebuild our bond, and we grew closer.

Steps to Rebuild Trust and Understanding

When family relationships feel fractured, there's still hope. The following steps can help rebuild trust and understanding with family members while ensuring honesty and mutual respect.

1. Share Your Perspective

While you don't owe anyone an explanation for your life choices, sharing your perspective with close family members can foster understanding, reduce tension, and help them respect your decisions.

When starting the conversation, frame it around your personal growth and well-being. Focus on how your decision comes after careful thought and the desire for a healthier and more fulfilling life.

For example, you might say:

- "I know my decision has been difficult for you to understand, but it's done. This is the best way for me to live a happier and healthier life."

- "This wasn't an easy choice for me either. I deeply appreciate your love and support as I start this new chapter."

Speaking openly and vulnerably may help your family see the situation from your perspective and soften any judgment or disappointment they may have.

2. Show Appreciation

Even when your family doesn't handle the situation well—whether by offering unsolicited advice, avoiding difficult conversations, or expressing frustration—acknowledge their efforts. Recognizing their attempts, even if imperfect, can help strengthen your relationship and encourage more constructive interactions. Expressing gratitude lets them know their presence in your life is valued.

To show appreciation, thank them for their support, even if it's imperfect. Acknowledge small gestures, like checking in or offering help. Let them know you value their efforts.

For example, you might say:

- "I know this hasn't been easy for everyone, and I appreciate that you're trying to be there for me. It means more than you know."

- "Thank you for listening to me and giving me the space to work through things. Your support means a lot to me."

3. Be Compassionate

As you adjust to this new life, your family is also trying to adapt. They may say the wrong things or make mistakes in their efforts to support you.

Be compassionate to those who are genuinely trying to help, but also recognize the difference between sincere support and behavior that may be harmful. Genuine support respects your boundaries and prioritizes your well-being, while toxic behaviors may involve guilt-tripping, constant criticism, or dismissing your emotions. Acknowledge those who offer positive encouragement, and don't hesitate to distance yourself from interactions that feel manipulative or unsupportive.

To offer compassion, assume positive intent, even if their actions feel misguided. Focus on their effort rather than their mistakes and communicate openly about what you need from them moving forward.

For instance, when my mom expressed frustration about how our family gatherings felt different after my marriage ended, I initially felt defensive. Later, I realized she was grieving the loss of the family dynamic we once shared. I acknowledged her feelings and reassured her that, while things had changed, I was still her son and committed to staying connected as a family.

4. Encourage Honest Communication

Building trust and understanding starts with honest communication. However, fear of conflict, past misunderstandings, or differing perspectives can make open dialogue challenging. To overcome these barriers, approach conversations with patience, actively listen without judgment and validate each other's emotions. Setting a safe and respectful space for discussion encourages more meaningful and productive exchanges.

To encourage honest communication:

- Choose a calm and private place for discussions.

- Use "I" statements to express your feelings without blaming anyone.

- Be patient and give others time to process and respond to what you've said.

For example, you might say:

- "I feel hurt when my decisions are questioned, but I also understand that this has been hard for you. I want us to work through this together."

5. Accept That Not Every Relationship Will Heal

Rebuilding family relationships after a divorce may be harder than you anticipated. Some relationships may never return to their previous state, while others may not require much effort before getting back on track. Accepting this reality can be difficult, but focusing on what you can control—such as setting boundaries, maintaining open communication, and prioritizing mutual respect—can help you find peace.

If a relationship does not fully heal, consider shifting your expectations and finding new ways to engage with that person in a way that feels healthy and sustainable for both of you. You aren't in control of everything, and what matters most is focusing on your growth and healing.

By following these steps, you'll be on the right track to mending fractured bonds and building stronger connections with family members. While your divorce may have re-shaped your family relationships, it's also an opportunity to redefine them in ways that nurture your well-being and bring you closer to the people who truly matter.

When and How to Start Dating Again (Without Rebounding)

The Pressure to Date Again

"When are you going to start dating again?"

This is one of the most common questions many divorced people are asked. It may be a well-meaning inquiry, but as the recipient, you may feel unnecessary pressure, which can slow down your recovery.

When I was asked, I initially felt annoyed and irritated. "Why wouldn't people just mind their business and let me be?" I wondered. But as I reflected, I realized that society often equates being in a relationship with being whole or successful. Over time, I stopped resenting the question and understood that their perspective didn't define my worth.

The Dangers of Rebounding

Getting into a relationship before healing can lead to rebound relationships that are often short-lived and emotionally draining. These relationships usually stem from a need for validation or distraction rather than genuine compatibility. Without processing past emotions, unresolved issues can surface, causing misunderstandings, insecurity, and instability. Ultimately, this cycle can leave individuals feeling even more unsettled than before.

I remember a close friend sharing her experience after her divorce. A few months after the separation, she started dating—not because she had found someone she genuinely connected with, but because everyone around her encouraged her to "put herself out there." She also wanted to prove to herself and others that she was still desirable.

Initially, the excitement of dating masked her pain. But as the honeymoon phase faded, unresolved emotions from her divorce resurfaced. Not long after, the relationship ended, making her feel even more lost than before. This is a common experience for many divorced individuals.

It's important to give yourself time to heal before seeking a new partner. Psychologists suggest that rebound relationships often act as coping mechanisms, temporarily masking pain and delaying true emotional recovery. Individuals who enter rebound relationships are more likely to experience lingering feelings of insecurity and frustration than those who take time to heal before dating again.

Signs You're Ready to Date

How do you know when you're truly ready to re-enter the dating world? Dating after divorce is a significant decision that requires emotional readiness and self-awareness. The goal isn't just to find someone new; it's to be in a good place to build a healthy connection without unresolved baggage. Here are key signs that show your readiness:

1. You're Comfortable Being Alone

Do you enjoy your own company? If you no longer seek someone to fill a void or validate your worth, you're in a healthier place to build a meaningful connection.

2. You've Processed the Past

If you've worked through intense emotions—such as anger, resentment, or lingering feelings about your ex—you're less likely to carry emotional baggage into a new relationship. This stage isn't easy to reach, but journaling, therapy, and introspection can help you get there.

3. You're Excited, Not Desperate

When the idea of dating no longer feels like a desperate attempt to avoid loneliness but a genuine interest in connecting with someone, you're likely ready. Dating should feel like a choice, not a necessity.

How to Approach Dating

Starting to date after divorce can be overwhelming due to changes in social norms, personal insecurities, and the fear of making the same mistakes. Navigating dating apps, understanding modern dating etiquette, and rebuilding confidence can add to the emotional weight of the experience. Where do you start? Have you healed? Do you have the mental capacity to go through this again? These are important questions to consider.

While some people may pressure you to move on, remember that re-entering the dating world is a deeply personal journey. There isn't a set timeline or strict rules for when and how to date. However, with certain strategies, you can approach dating with a mindset of growth, self-respect, and emotional readiness.

1. Take It Slow

Start with casual outings like coffee dates or evening walks. Low-pressure settings allow you to get to know someone without the weight of high expectations. My first date after my divorce was a coffee meet-up. We discussed books, travel, and life experiences without diving into heavy topics. It was refreshing and gave me the confidence to explore connections at a comfortable pace.

2. Be Honest

Transparency is key in any relationship. Your potential date should know where you are emotionally and what you're looking for. If you're not ready for a serious commitment, communicate that early on.

3. Check for Compatibility

Physical attraction and charm can easily capture your attention when dating, but it's equally important to prioritize shared values, interests, and goals. While initial chemistry is exciting, true compatibility is built on deeper alignment rather than surface-level qualities.

Overcoming Fear of Vulnerability

After my divorce, I struggled with dating due to fear of vulnerability. I worried about opening up again, fearing rejection and emotional pain. However, through self-reflection and taking time to heal, I gradually rebuilt my confidence. When I finally felt ready, I approached dating cautiously, allowing myself to take small steps toward meaningful connections.

One of my first experiences was meeting someone for coffee who shared my love for reading. We bonded over mutual interests and had candid conversations about our past experiences. The relationship was a positive and respectful experience, showing me that I was capable of forming genuine connections again.

Re-entering the dating world after divorce is both an emotional and practical journey. There's no rush to move on. Take the time to heal, rediscover your strengths, and build a life that feels fulfilling on your own terms. When you do choose to date again, do so from a place of self-awareness and resilience—this will lay the foundation for a relationship that truly enhances your life.

Avoiding the Rebound Trap

Recognizing a Rebound Relationship

Have you ever been in a relationship that moved too fast, with intense emotions developing almost immediately? In such relationships, you may feel like you're seeking an escape from loneliness rather than pursuing a genuine connection. Instead of focusing on building a strong foundation, you may be more concerned with proving something to yourself or others. If this sounds familiar, you may have experienced a rebound relationship.

Rebound relationships can be tempting because they provide a temporary boost to self-esteem and offer a distraction from emotional pain. However, they can also prevent you from fully healing, leaving you emotionally unprepared for a meaningful connection in the future.

Prioritizing Self-Growth

To avoid falling into the rebound trap, prioritize self-growth before entering a new relationship. Use this time to explore hobbies, develop skills, and pursue goals that enhance your sense of identity. Surround yourself with supportive relationships—such as family and friends—that fulfill your emotional needs without the pressure of romantic involvement.

Seeking Professional Support

If needed, seek therapy to help process lingering emotions and recognize unhealthy patterns from past relationships. A professional can offer valuable insights into your relationship dynamics, helping you identify behaviors to avoid in the future. Therapy also fosters self-awareness, allowing you to make healthier relationship choices and enter future connections with confidence and emotional stability.

Healthy relationships should encourage mutual respect, shared growth, and emotional support. For this to happen, both partners must enter the relationship with a sense of wholeness and a willingness to contribute equally.

Building a Foundation for Healthy Love

The Value of Friendship First

Start with friendship to build a solid foundation for healthy love. Some of the strongest relationships develop from genuine friendships—two colleagues bonding over shared interests, for instance, before realizing their romantic potential. Taking the time to understand someone in a platonic way first fosters a deeper emotional connection and trust, laying the groundwork for a lasting relationship. Clear and honest communication is essential, setting the stage for trust and mutual understanding.

The Importance of Non-Transactional Relationships

Have you heard of the concept of non-transactional relationships? These are connections built on genuine care rather than what each person can gain from the other. Examples include a friend who checks in simply because they care about you—not because they expect something in return. Or a family member who supports your decisions without imposing their own opinions. Meaningful relationships are based on valuing a person for who they are rather than for how they meet your needs.

Research supports the idea that non-transactional relationships improve emotional well-being. Individuals who prioritize intrinsic relationship values—such as emotional intimacy and mutual respect—report higher levels of satisfaction and lower levels of anxiety in their connections.

By prioritizing non-transactional relationships, you create space for connections that enrich your life. This approach not only improves your romantic life but also strengthens friendships and family bonds, fostering deeper fulfillment in all aspects of your relationships.

By reconnecting with old friends, navigating family dynamics, and approaching dating with intention, you can create a support system that uplifts and adds value to your life. The most meaningful relationships are rooted in mutual respect and understanding—not in desperation or convenience.

Chapter Key Points

- Divorce can affect family relationships, but it also presents an opportunity to redefine them.

- Set boundaries to protect your emotional well-being and encourage healthier interactions.

- Show gratitude for your family's support, even if they have flaws and imperfections—this can strengthen your bond with them.

- Emotional readiness is key to re-entering the dating world. Feeling comfortable alone, processing your past, and approaching dating with excitement rather than desperation are strong indicators of readiness.

- Take a slow, intentional approach to dating. Start with low-pressure outings and focus on compatibility rather than surface-level qualities.

- Avoid falling into the rebound trap, as these relationships often lack emotional depth and hinder long-term emotional growth.

Chapter Five

Regaining Stability:

Financial, Legal, and Physical Well-being

"Do not dwell in the past, do not dream of the future, concentrate the mind on the present moment."

- Buddha

Rebuilding Stability After Divorce

"How can I rebuild a foundation that feels steady beneath my feet?" I asked myself as I sat on my bed one quiet evening, wondering what stability feels or looks like.

Before me was a stack of unopened bills and a scantily written to-do list, each item a stark reminder of the responsibilities I had been avoiding. The sight of them sent a wave of anxiety through me, a physical weight settling in my chest as I struggled to summon the motivation to face what lay ahead. I felt lost, unsure of where to go from there. I wanted stability so badly, but it felt impossible to get it back.

My once-clear plans for the future had become a blur of uncertainty, and it seemed like everything needed fixing at the same time. There were cracks in my financial, legal, and even physical well-being.

I vividly remember the moment I realized I had to stop reacting to the mess and start taking charge. My longtime friend Mark had asked me, "If you could change one thing right now, what would it be?" That question hit me hard because, truthfully, I didn't know where to start. Should I tackle the growing pile of paperwork? Address the sinking feeling in my gut when I thought about the future? Or find a way to regain the strength I felt slipping away?

At first, I tried to do it all. I overcompensated, thinking that if I fixed everything at once, I'd feel like myself again. I signed up for a gym membership, created a budget spreadsheet, and scheduled every spare moment of my time to get back on track. But all it did was leave me feeling more overwhelmed. I wasn't addressing the root of the instability—the fear of financial insecurity, unresolved legal concerns, and my declining physical well-being. Instead, I was applying temporary patches to deep cracks, hoping they wouldn't widen further.

Then came the turning point. One night, after failing to power through yet another exhausting day, I sat down and wrote a list of the areas I needed to rebuild: my financial security, my physical strength, and my legal issues. I realized I needed to approach these areas one at a time. I stopped trying to fix everything at once and created a plan that prioritized what mattered most.

As I began to take small, intentional steps, I started to notice progress. I worked on setting up a budget that wasn't just about cutting costs but one that gave me peace of mind. I sought professional advice to clarify my legal rights, which lifted a huge mental weight. Instead of pressuring myself to hit the gym five times a week, I focused on engaging in simple physical habits that made me feel stronger. The plan wasn't perfect, but progress was the goal.

Rebuilding stability after divorce means recognizing the key pillars of your well-being: financial, legal, and physical health. It requires committing to steady, manageable progress in each area, focusing on one step at a time. Don't try to solve everything at once—take it one step at a time.

Managing Finances After Divorce: Budgeting and Saving

When I first faced life after my divorce, I had to confront the harsh reality of how little I knew about my finances. My ex had always managed the household budget while I focused on other areas. Suddenly, I was solely in charge of bills, managing debts, and trying to plan for an unpredictable future. It was overwhelming, but it was also a wake-up call.

Divorce often shakes our entire foundation, leaving us to rebuild from scratch. I remember standing in my half-empty apartment, surrounded by boxes I couldn't bring myself to unpack, feeling like a stranger in my own life. The silence was deafening, and the uncertainty ahead felt paralyzing. In that moment, I realized I had to start over—not just physically but emotionally and financially as well. We must divide assets, adjust to a single income, or downsize our lifestyle. It's challenging, but don't let all your hard work over the years go down the drain. Pick up what's left, take control, and create financial stability for the future.

Rebuilding your finances after a divorce can feel very overwhelming. Where do you even start? I've been there, and I promise it gets better. Here's what worked for me and many others picking up the pieces.

1. Face the Numbers, Even When They're Scary

The first step is to take a hard look at your finances—your income, expenses, debts, and assets. I remember sitting at my office desk, surrounded by unopened bank statements, my laptop glaring at me, and a half-eaten burger nearby. My hands shook as I finally cracked open those envelopes I'd been avoiding for weeks. It was messy and emotional, but it was also the first time I felt in control.

I started scribbling down everything—my income, bills, debts, and even a dusty old savings account I'd forgotten about. I quickly realized I was wasting money on unused subscriptions. Why was I paying for three streaming services? And those daily takeouts added up to the cost of a small vacation.

As I dug deeper, I discovered a hidden credit card debt I didn't even know existed. Writing down every single debt, even the random medical bill from two years ago, gave me clarity. It wasn't easy, but at least I knew what I was up against.

Now it's your turn. Turn on the lights in your financial life and see exactly where you stand. Pick up a notebook or use a budgeting app to lay everything bare—your income, bills, debts, and even that gym membership you swore you'd use.

2. Create a Budget That Works for You

Once you know where you stand, it's time to create a budget. I started with non-negotiables like rent, utilities, and groceries, then worked backward. Cutting out my daily coffee shop runs and impulse buys felt brutal at first, but it freed me. For the first time, I wasn't wondering where my paycheck went every month.

You don't have to use complex spreadsheets—budgeting apps, sticky notes, or simple lists work too. Start with essentials before moving to flexible expenses. Leave room for yourself because a budget that's too strict will backfire. I was too hard on myself at first and soon relapsed into 2 a.m. online shopping.

Don't make the same mistake—keep your budget realistic! If it's too restrictive, you'll end up feeling frustrated. Allow yourself small splurges like a dinner out once a month or an item you've always wanted. Just plan for it!

3. Build an Emergency Fund

One of the biggest lessons I learned from my divorce was the importance of an emergency fund. Life will throw unexpected expenses at you, and Being financially ready can have a significant impact.

My wake-up call was a flooded basement five months post-split. Standing ankle-deep in water, I realized I had nothing saved for emergencies. The panic spiral was real. That's when I vowed to start saving, even on a tight budget.

At first, it felt impossible, but I set up an automatic transfer of $100 from each paycheck into a dedicated savings account. It didn't seem like much, but those small contributions added up.

Six months later, when my car unexpectedly broke down, I breathed a sigh of relief. Instead of panicking, I tapped into my savings. A wave of relief washed over me—I was prepared. I felt empowered, no longer at the mercy of unexpected expenses but in control of my financial future.

Experts suggest saving 3 to 6 months' worth of expenses, but don't let that number scare you. Start small—even saving $50 a month can provide a cushion in an emergency. The goal is to take the first step toward building your safety net.

Smart Saving Strategies

Saving money isn't about earning a high income, but about developing smart financial habits. Even if you make thousands of dollars each month, without a solid savings plan, you might find yourself running out of funds before the month is over. The key is to be intentional with how you manage your money. Through personal experience, I've learned valuable strategies that have transformed my financial stability, and I'd love to share them with you.

Automate Your Savings

One of the most effective ways to save is to automate the process. When I realized how crucial this was, I arranged automatic transfers from my checking account to my savings account every payday. At first, it was uncomfortable because I was used to spending every cent of my paycheck. But I treated savings like a non-negotiable bill that had to be paid. Over time, I hardly noticed the difference, and my savings steadily grew in the background. By automating your savings, you make it effortless and sustainable.

Cut Non-Essential Expenses

I remember sitting down with my bank statements and scrutinizing my spending habits. I found subscriptions—streaming services, magazine memberships, and gym member-ships—I hadn't used in months. Canceling them saved me a significant amount of money.

By eliminating non-essential expenses, such as daily coffee shop visits, impulse purchases, or unused memberships, you can lighten your budget and boost your savings effortlessly.

Negotiate Your Bills

Many people don't realize that some bills are negotiable. One day, on a whim, I called my internet provider to ask if there were any promotions available. To my surprise, they immediately offered me a discount, saving me $20 a month!

Negotiate the bills you can, such as internet, phone plans, insurance, and even rent in some cases. There's no harm in asking, and you might be pleasantly surprised by the savings you secure.

Embrace Meal Prepping

A significant portion of monthly expenses often goes toward food, especially dining out. While convenient, it can drain your budget quickly. I decided to cook at home more often and started meal prepping. Initially, it felt like a chore, but over time, I found it enjoyable. I experimented with new recipes and planned my meals ahead. The result? I saved over $300 a month!

Utilize Technology

Budgeting apps can revolutionize the way you track your spending and savings goals. Apps like Mint and YNAB (You Need a Budget) provide easy-to-use tools to manage finances effectively. Even a simple spreadsheet can help you monitor your expenses and savings. The key is to find a system that works for you and stick to it.

Seek Financial Guidance

When things get tough, and you feel overwhelmed, don't hesitate to seek help. Many local resources, such as libraries and community centers, offer free financial planning workshops. Talking to financially savvy loved ones can also provide valuable insights and encouragement.

Small Changes Lead to Big Results

Every small decision adds up. Whether it's canceling an unused subscription, setting up automated savings, or cooking at home, each choice you make moves you closer to financial stability. Take control of your finances to create a strong foundation for a brighter and more secure future. That sense of control is one of the most liberating feelings you'll ever experience.

The Importance of a Strong Support Network: Legal and Emotional

Going through a divorce is a challenging and emotionally taxing experience. Between property division, custody agreements, and financial settlements, the process can quickly become overwhelming. Having the right support—both legal and emotional—can make all the difference in navigating this transition successfully.

Legal Support: Why It Matters

Hiring a good attorney who specializes in family law can be your most valuable asset, especially one with a strong track record in handling cases similar to yours. Look for someone who is knowledgeable about state-specific laws and skilled in negotiation and litigation, ensuring they can effectively advocate for your best interests.

During my search for legal counsel, I met with three different attorneys before finding someone who truly understood my situation. My lawyer not only explained the legal process in clear terms but also made me feel heard and prioritized. For example, when I was worried about securing a fair custody arrangement for my kids, she took the time to calmly explain my options and what the courts typically look for in such cases. Knowing I had someone fighting for my interests while keeping me informed made a world of difference.

At the start of the divorce process, legal support is crucial for understanding your rights and securing a fair outcome. As the process unfolds, emotional support from family and friends or professional counselors can help you manage stress and maintain stability. In the later stages, practical support, such as co-parenting guidance or financial planning advice, becomes invaluable for transitioning into your new life.

Legal Strategies to Keep in Mind

- **Hire an Experienced Attorney** – Look for someone who specializes in family law and aligns with your goals. During consultations, ask questions to understand their approach and past cases.

- **Know Your Rights** – Familiarize yourself with the laws in your area regarding property division, custody, and spousal support. Knowing your rights will allow you to make better decisions throughout the process.

- **Document Everything** – Keep meticulous records of financial transactions, communications with your ex, and any agreements. A detailed record can clarify custody disputes and ensure that you aren't overlooked in financial settlements.

Emotional Support: Your Anchor in Difficult Times

Divorce can be an isolating experience, making it important to lean on those who offer empathy and genuine support. While a good attorney guides you through the legal aspects of your divorce, an emotional support network serves as your anchor in difficult times.

During my divorce, I found solace in Dave, a childhood friend who had always been a steady presence in my life. He reminded me of the importance of self-care. Whenever I felt overwhelmed, he'd invite me over for lunch or suggest going on hikes to talk through my feelings. These moments weren't just about venting—I felt genuinely understood and supported.

If you're not comfortable sharing your emotions with friends or family, consider joining a divorce support group. These groups can serve as a lifeline, connecting you with others who understand the challenges you're facing. A colleague of mine took this route after his divorce, and he found not only emotional comfort but also practical co-parenting advice that made his life easier.

The Balance Between Legal and Emotional Support

While your lawyer is focused on protecting your rights, your emotional network helps you rebuild your sense of self.

Know when to set boundaries, as not everyone in your life will respect your emotions or provide the support you need. For example, I had a family member who constantly gave unsolicited advice, leaving me more stressed than before. Eventually, I learned to limit those interactions and prioritize relationships that genuinely uplifted me.

Divorce is a major life transformation that impacts every aspect of your well-being. Surround yourself with people who understand what you're going through and are committed to supporting your transition holistically.

Finding Strength in Both Areas

After my divorce, I worked closely with my lawyer to secure a fair settlement, but I was emotionally drained. I needed balance, so I turned to a counselor who specialized in divorce recovery. Initially, I thought I was strong enough to handle everything alone, but I was wrong. Talking with a counselor helped me process my emotions, regain confidence, and approach legal negotiations with a clearer mindset.

This journey gave me firsthand experience of the need for both legal and emotional support to navigate the divorce process smoothly. A strong legal team protects your future, while an emotional network helps you heal and grow.

Divorce is intricate and requires a multifaceted approach to address both legal and emotional challenges. You don't have to face this storm alone. By finding the right combination of legal expertise and emotional support, you'll emerge stronger and ready to embrace the next chapter of your life. The right lawyer ensures you're protecting your interests while cultivating a strong emotional support network helps you regain balance and clarity.

Physical Health: Exercise and Well-Being as a Key to Mental Clarity

Divorce is emotionally and physically exhausting. During such a turbulent time, it's easy to neglect your physical well-being while focusing on legal and emotional struggles. Many months after my separation, I barely paid attention to my body's needs. My diet consisted of processed foods and coffee, and my sleep schedule was erratic. I convinced myself that I was too overwhelmed to prioritize my health.

But my energy levels were at an all-time low. I felt constantly fatigued, lacked motivation, and had no appetite. At one point, I feared I had a serious illness. A visit to the doctor, however, revealed that my poor habits were to blame. The doctor urged me to prioritize a balanced diet, regular exercise, and proper rest. He stressed that neglecting my body would only worsen my emotional struggles. His words struck a chord, and I resolved to rebuild my physical health—not just for my appearance, but for my well-being and ability to function.

Taking care of your physical health after divorce is not a luxury; it's a necessity. Exercise, healthy eating, and mind-body practices can help you regain mental clarity and emotional balance during this chaotic time.

The Link Between Physical and Mental Health

The stress of divorce often manifests in physical symptoms like headaches, insomnia, muscle tension, and fatigue. These are not coincidental—they reflect the deep connection between physical and mental well-being.

Exercise is not just for weight loss or muscle gain. It is a powerful tool for managing stress and enhancing mental clarity. When you exercise, your body releases endorphins—natural mood boosters that help reduce anxiety and stress. Studies have shown that regular physical activity can alleviate symptoms of depression and improve overall mood.

After my divorce, I struggled to find motivation. One morning, despite feeling drained, I laced up my running shoes and went for a jog. It was slow and brief, but as I felt my blood pumping and breathed in the fresh air, I realized how much I had missed that feeling. When I returned home, I committed to prioritizing my physical health. The benefits went beyond my fitness—I regained a sense of control over my life.

Prioritizing your body will create ripple effects in other areas of your life. Improved physical health leads to mental clarity, higher energy levels, and greater emotional resilience to face life's challenges with confidence.

Creating a Fitness Routine

Starting a fitness routine may feel overwhelming, especially when everything else in your life feels uncertain. The key is to begin small, choose activities you enjoy, and set realistic goals.

1. Start Small

If the idea of a gym intimidates you, start with something simple—like a short daily walk.

A friend of mine, John, was unsure where to start with fitness. He had never been particularly active and felt overwhelmed by all the conflicting advice online. Eventually, he began by taking short walks with his dog every evening. Over time, those walks turned into jogs, and he eventually joined a local running group that provided both fitness and community support.

2. Choose Activities You Enjoy

Not everyone enjoys running or weightlifting. Find a form of movement that excites you—whether it's swimming, hiking, dancing, or yoga. Choose an activity that feels less like a chore and more like therapy.

Initially, I dismissed yoga as "not for me." But once I tried it, I realized how much it helped both my body and my mind. It became a space where I could rebuild my strength while finding mental calmness.

3. Set Realistic Goals

The goal isn't perfection; it's consistency. Don't pressure yourself to exercise daily or feel guilty if you miss a session. Aim for three to four workouts per week and gradually increase intensity as you build momentum.

Choosing Healthy Eating for Energy and Clarity

What you eat directly affects how you feel—both physically and emotionally. Stress often leads to cravings for sugary snacks and caffeine, but these provide only temporary relief and leave you feeling sluggish and irritable.

I was guilty of this. I relied on takeout and instant meals, convincing myself that cooking for one wasn't worth the effort. However, after realizing how much my diet affected my energy levels and mental clarity, I made small changes—incorporating whole grains, lean proteins, and vegetables. The difference was immediate and profound.

To start eating healthier:

- **Plan balanced meals** with complex carbohydrates like brown rice and quinoa, lean proteins like fish and chicken, and plenty of vegetables.

- **Snack smart.** Keep nuts, yogurt, or fruit on hand to avoid reaching for junk food.

- **Limit caffeine and sugar intake.** While they offer quick energy boosts, they lead to crashes that leave you feeling worse.

I started preparing simple meals, like baked salmon with steamed broccoli and sweet potatoes. The goal wasn't gourmet cooking—it was fueling my body with real nutrients instead of fast food.

Consider creating a weekly meal and exercise plan. Writing it down or tracking it in an app can keep you accountable and motivated. Seeing your progress builds confidence and makes healthy habits easier to maintain.

Mind-Body Practices for Stress Relief

Beyond diet and exercise, incorporating practices like meditation, yoga, and quality sleep can significantly improve both physical and mental well-being.

1. Meditation

A few minutes of deep breathing daily can have a profound impact on stress levels. If you're new to meditation, apps like Calm or **Headspace** offer guided sessions to help you get started. When I first tried meditation, I struggled to quiet my racing thoughts. But over time, I found that even short sessions helped me feel more centered and in control.

2. Mindful Movement

Yoga and tai chi blend movement with mindfulness, reducing stress while improving flexibility, balance, and strength. These practices are excellent for those looking to reconnect with their bodies in a gentle way.

3. Quality Sleep

Sleep is important for both your physical and mental health. Aim for 7–8 hours each night, maintain a consistent bedtime, and limit screen time before bed. Establishing a relaxing nighttime routine—such as reading a book or drinking herbal tea—can significantly improve sleep quality.

Reclaiming Your Strength and Independence

By addressing your financial, legal, and physical well-being, you're taking a stand to create a secure and purposeful life. This journey is about rediscovering your strength, reclaiming your independence, and building a future you can look forward to.

Chapter Key Points:

- Assess your financial situation and create a solid financial plan.

- Rebuild financial security by budgeting, cutting unnecessary expenses, and setting savings goals.

- Secure legal protection—consult an attorney, understand your rights, and document agreements.

- Strengthen your body and mind through regular exercise, nutritious meals, and good sleep habits.

- Build a reliable support system—lean on trusted friends, family, or professional advisors.

- Take proactive steps toward growth—set clear goals, develop new skills, and make intentional choices that create a stable and fulfilling future.

Every small decision you make contributes to your healing and strength. Take control of your well-being, one step at a time.

Chapter Six

Moving from Surviving to Thriving:

Rebuilding Your Life After ivorce

"Rock bottom became the solid foundation on which I rebuilt my life."
- J.K. Rowling

Acknowledging Where You Are

I know things might feel overwhelming right now, like you're carrying a heavy weight every day. You may feel stuck, with each day blurring into the next, focused solely on making it through bedtime. Your life has been turned upside down, leaving you to navigate difficult emotions, heartache, and new responsibilities. You're going through the motions, trying to hold everything together while parts of your spirit feel like they're slipping away.

If any of this sounds familiar, you're in survival mode. This phase can be exhausting because you aren't truly living—you're merely existing.

Survival mode is a natural response to adversity, where your focus is on simply getting through each day. While this phase is necessary for coping, it can leave you feeling drained and disconnected from true fulfillment. However, survival mode shouldn't be the end of your story. Life has more to offer than just getting by. You can move from surviving to actually thriving if you set your mind to it. Small, intentional steps can lead you to a happier and brighter future.

My Moment of Awakening

I certainly remember my moment of awakening—a time when I realized that merely getting through the day wasn't enough. Like you, I had been struggling, feeling weighed down by expectations and responsibilities. That realization became my turning point, nudging me toward a life with more meaning.

For a long time, I lived in a cycle of heartache, overwhelmed by the pressure to keep up appearances and manage responsibilities I hadn't anticipated. Functioning became my norm, but I wasn't truly living. Eventually, I allowed myself to hope again—even if it was just a little at first. That small hope nudged me toward something better.

That is what this chapter is all about. It will guide you in moving beyond mere survival to discovering what's possible. Just like a seed buried in darkness eventually pushes through to reach the sunlight, you, too, can grow into something great after this tough phase. Through small and intentional changes, you'll learn to identify what excites you, set meaningful goals, and create the life you've been hoping for.

The Importance of Acknowledgment

Before we get started, take this moment to acknowledge where you are right now. Are you waking up each day just trying to get through? If so, that's entirely valid. Survival mode is a natural reaction to a significant loss—like your divorce. It's your brain's way of helping you cope with overwhelm. However, staying in that mode for too long can weigh you down and trap you in a cycle that convinces you this is all there is.

You may not have control over everything that has happened, but you do have control over how you respond moving forward. Choose to transition from merely surviving to thriving.

Identifying Personal Passions and Setting New Goals

For many years, you may have strongly identified with the role of a husband or father, shaping much of your daily life and priorities. It may feel like you've been wearing a uniform for so long that you've forgotten how to take it off. Now that you're divorced, this is an opportunity to shed that uniform and rediscover who you truly are.

Ask yourself these important questions:

- What lights me up?

- What do I really want for myself?

- Who am I outside of the role of being a husband and father?

Reconnecting with yourself after a divorce is no easy feat. It can feel like a total reset with no clear path forward. But you can start by rediscovering what makes you uniquely you, and together, we will take small and meaningful steps to achieve this.

1. Unearth the Real You—He's Still in There

Psychologists often discuss the concept of "self-concept clarity," which refers to how well we know ourselves, including our interests, values, and preferences. However, a life-changing event like a divorce can blur this sense of self. Research shows that in long-term relationships, partners often merge identities, sharing hobbies, social circles, and routines. When the relationship ends, it can leave you wondering: What parts of your life were truly yours?

You can rebuild your sense of self by reflecting on past joys, engaging in new experiences, and exploring different roles.

Think of this phase as an opportunity to update your personal "operating system." You're not erasing your past but rather enhancing it, incorporating lessons that will lead to a better version of yourself.

2. Identify Your Interests

Let's take a trip down memory lane. Do you remember the time before your marriage when life was free of juggling responsibilities and compromises? What were the activities you enjoyed? Was it writing, exercising, hiking, watching movies, or painting?

For me, I've always loved journaling. I used to put my thoughts on paper, but during my marriage, life got busy, and my journals collected dust. After my divorce, I found my way back to journaling. I picked up a pen again and started writing, rediscovering something that had always brought me joy.

If you're struggling to remember your passions, that's okay. Start small by making a list of the things that once interested you. Commit to exploring just one or two of them before adding more. Don't overthink it or be hard on yourself—sometimes, the act of trying alone is more important than the result.

3. Find New Experiences

This is the stage where you experiment! Try different things and see what resonates with you. If there's something you've always wanted to do but have been putting off, now is the time to try it.

When I was rediscovering myself, I decided to try yoga. I never thought of myself as a "yoga person" and assumed it was mainly for women. But something about it intrigued me, so I enrolled in a class. The first few sessions were awkward—I couldn't touch my toes, and my downward dog looked more like a lazy cat. But over time, I found that yoga didn't just stretch my body—it stretched my mind, teaching me patience and self-compassion.

Find what works for you and makes you happy. If something doesn't stick, it's not a failure; it's just one more step toward understanding yourself. Every small effort brings you closer to the person you're meant to become.

4. Set Goals That Actually Stick

Goals will give you direction and a sense of purpose. Now that you've explored your interests and reconnected with what excites you, it's time to turn that energy into tangible goals. It's important to remember that not all goals are created equal, and that's why you need to make them SMART.

SMART is an acronym that stands for Specific, Measurable, Achievable, Relevant, and Time-bound. Here's how you can set goals that stick:

- **Specific**: Be clear on what you want to achieve. Instead of saying, "I want to get fit," make it specific—"I want to run a 5K in three months."

- **Measurable**: Define how you'll track progress. If you are learning a new skill, start with a beginner's course and track your improvement over time.

- **Achievable**: Set realistic goals. If you haven't exercised in years, don't aim for 100 push-ups daily—start with a manageable number and build up.

- **Relevant**: Align your goals with your values and long-term vision. Instead of vaguely saying, "I want to improve my finances," set a goal like, "I will save $500 monthly by reducing unnecessary expenses."

- **Time-bound**: Establish deadlines to create urgency and accountability. For example, "I will save $500 monthly for the next 12 months."

5. Use The "5-Minute Rule" to Overcome Procrastination

You've probably heard the saying, "How do you eat an elephant? One bite at a time." This principle is crucial when tackling overwhelming tasks. Big changes start small.

Using the "5-Minute Rule" means committing to just 5 minutes a day on your goal, helping to reduce resistance and making progress feel more manageable. You don't need to dive into an all-consuming commitment—just start small. Want to exercise, learn a new skill, or start a business? Dedicate five minutes daily, and you'll see real progress over time.

For example, if you want to establish a workout routine, don't force yourself into a rigid gym schedule. Start with a 5-minute walk. Once you consistently do it, it becomes easier to extend it to 10, 15, or even 30 minutes. The key is simply beginning.

Starting is often the hardest part. A mental block can make even the smallest tasks feel daunting, but once you get over that initial hurdle, momentum takes over. That five-minute effort could eventually lead to a sustainable and rewarding habit.

Finding Joy and Purpose in Everyday Life

Divorce can sometimes leave you feeling like your days lack excitement and meaning, but it doesn't have to stay that way. You may believe that thriving is reserved for monumental moments—landing a dream job, buying a house, or falling in love again. But the truth is, thriving often begins in the quiet, unassuming moments of everyday life.

Taking in the sunset after a long day, savoring a sip of coffee in the morning, and laughing at a friend's silly joke might seem insignificant. However, these small moments contribute to long-term happiness by grounding you in the present, providing comfort, and reinforcing the beauty in daily life. Joy is not something you have to wait for—it can meet you exactly where you are.

Research in positive psychology highlights the power of small wins. Dr. Teresa Amabile of Harvard Business School found that celebrating incremental progress significantly boosts motivation and emotional well-being.

Your small wins should serve as stepping stones across a river, helping you navigate uncertain waters with each step forward. Some stones may be sturdy and easy to cross, while others might feel wobbly, but each one is a testament to your progress and resilience. Even if some steps feel shaky, they still move you forward toward the other side.

Cultivating Everyday Joy

During my divorce, I remember feeling overwhelmed by the big picture. "How was I supposed to build a happy and fulfilling life when I could barely get through the day?" I'd always ask myself.

But when I started focusing on small wins, I was reminded that progress, no matter how small, can bring joy. I shifted my focus from grand gestures and life-altering changes to appreciating the significance of small, everyday moments. It started with noticing and nurturing the small joys already present in my life. One day, it was as simple as organizing my workspace. Another day, I was making myself a healthy meal instead of grabbing fast food.

How to Cultivate Everyday Joy

Practice Gratitude

Gratitude is a proven way to rewire your brain. Studies have shown that practicing gratitude can increase happiness levels, reduce stress, and even improve overall physical health. Gratitude shifts your perspective from what's lacking to what's meaningful.

At the end of each day, write down three things you're grateful for. It could be the way the sunlight filtered through the trees during your morning walk or the unexpected kindness of a stranger holding the door for you. Over time, you'll find yourself noticing the beauty and abundance already present in your life.

Be Present

Do you often rush through your days, barely noticing the moments that make them up? Mindfulness can help you slow down and truly savor life.

I remember the first time I truly practiced mindfulness. I was walking through a park, distracted by a million thoughts, when I decided to pause and be present. I took off my shoes and focused on the crunch of leaves under my feet, the warmth of the sun on my skin, and the rhythmic sound of birds chirping. It might have seemed unusual to others, but for the first time in months, I felt truly connected to the moment.

The next time you're outside, pause and notice the sensations, sounds, or even colors around you. When having a cup of coffee, take a few deep breaths and really savor the aroma and taste.

Celebrate Your Wins

One of the most empowering lessons I've learned after my divorce is the importance of celebrating progress, no matter how small. Did you finally tackle the pile of dirty dishes?

That's a win! Did you make it through a tough day at work without snapping? Another win!

Acknowledging these little victories helps you build confidence and momentum. Over time, you will create a positive feedback loop; a small step forward makes you capable of doing more.

Living with Purpose

It took me years to fully understand that purpose isn't something you find; you create it. It's in the way you choose to show up each day, the relationships you nurture, and the values you live by.

Transitioning from celebrating small wins to discovering a deeper sense of purpose was a journey in itself. Finding purpose after my divorce wasn't easy. As a divorced father of two, I struggled a lot; I felt lost and unsure of who I was. Most of the time, finding a purpose felt like searching for a needle in a haystack. It was only after talking with my therapist that I realized I didn't need to have all the answers. The goal was simply to create a life aligned with my values and desires.

Finding my purpose started with understanding what truly mattered to me. I realized that helping others, whether through small acts of kindness or bigger commitments, gave me a sense of fulfillment I couldn't find anywhere else. Giving back to my community reminded me of my own resilience. Through that process, I rediscovered my ability to create positive change, both in my life and in the lives of others.

Your purpose doesn't need to be grand. Sometimes, just showing up and making a difference in small but meaningful ways is enough. Now, I ask you—what kind of man do you want to be? What legacy do you want to leave behind? What impact do you want to have on others?

Your purpose doesn't have to be tied to your career or one aspect of your life. It can be as multifaceted as you are. You can find purpose in the smallest things that bring you joy, in your strength and how you use it to help others, and in the kind of life you want to create for yourself and those around you.

Purpose isn't about waiting for the perfect moment—it's about embracing the present and making it meaningful.

Creating a Thriving Future, Not Just a "Getting By" Existence

The life you've spent years building is gone, and now you're left to sift through the rubble. During this phase, it's easy to fall into a mindset of simply "getting by" surviving day-to-day without a clear direction.

What if I told you that your life doesn't need to be a half-hearted existence? Stop "getting by." Instead, rebuild your life and create a future that reflects your desires.

It's time to envision a life that excites you and take deliberate steps to turn that vision into reality.

Visualizing Your Ideal Life

My dad always said, "If you don't know where you're going, any road will take you there." It took me a long time to realize the power of that statement. To thrive in life, you need a clear vision of what you want it to look like.

Psychological studies show that visualizing success improves your chances of achieving it. Neurologically, the brain begins to treat that vision as reality and motivates you to take action.

Here's a quick exercise to help you visualize your ideal life:

Imagine that your fears and self-doubts aren't holding you back. What would your ideal day look like? Would you wake up early for a run, spend the afternoon working on a project you love, or end the day with laughter and good conversation among friends?

Write your answers with as much detail as possible to make your vision clearer. What time do you wake up? Where are you living? What are you doing for work, fun, or relaxation? Who do you want to spend your time with?

This exercise isn't just wishful thinking—it can serve as a blueprint for your future. Visualizing my ideal life after a difficult transition wasn't easy. I was stuck in a cycle of doubt, constantly replaying what I'd lost instead of imagining what I could gain. But once I allowed myself to dream, everything changed. Writing down what I wanted helped me focus on the possibilities rather than the obstacles.

Key Steps to Build a Thriving Future

1. Invest in Yourself

Investing in yourself is the foundation for growth. Humans are like gardens; to thrive, they need care, nourishment, and the removal of obstacles that hinder growth. Whether it's picking up a new skill, prioritizing your physical health, or exploring new careers, every step you take toward self-improvement is a step toward thriving.

I knew a guy who had always loved woodworking but never pursued it. After his divorce, he decided to give it a shot. He started small—watching YouTube tutorials and working on projects in his garage. Over time, he honed his skills, and now he sells custom-made furniture in his local community. It's amazing what happens when you nurture your passions.

Have you always wanted to learn something new? Take an online course, enroll in a workshop, or read books that challenge your thinking. Growth doesn't happen by chance—it's an intentional process.

Take care of your body and mind. Eat well, exercise regularly, and make time for rest. Explore emotional and spiritual growth. Journaling, meditation, or therapy can help you uncover what truly matters to you.

2. Build Resilience

Resilience is your ability to adapt, learn, and grow in the face of adversity. Life will throw challenges your way. But thriving doesn't mean avoiding hardship—it means navigating it with strength.

Resilience often starts with a mindset rooted in growth and adaptability. Embracing a growth mindset—where challenges are seen as opportunities to learn—can significantly impact your ability to thrive. Cultivating adaptability ensures that you can adjust to unexpected changes without feeling defeated.

Instead of fearing failure, use it as an opportunity to learn. Each setback is a lesson guiding you forward. Life rarely goes according to plan, so be open to change and flexible in finding new paths when the old ones no longer work.

When I lost my job, I felt like my world was collapsing. But instead of giving up, I used it as an opportunity to pivot. I returned to school, earned new certifications, and landed better jobs than before.

3. Surround Yourself with Positive Influences

The people you spend time with shape how you think and behave. Surrounding yourself with positive, supportive individuals can make a world of difference as you rebuild your life.

Join groups or communities that match your interests—whether it's a hiking club, a professional network, or an online support group. The goal is to connect with like-minded people who encourage and support you.

Seek out mentors who are thriving in ways you admire. Their guidance and motivation can be invaluable as you work toward your goals. Thriving requires emotional space to focus on what truly matters, so avoid toxic relationships that drain your energy.

After my divorce, I realized many of my friendships were built around negativity and complaining. I made a conscious decision to distance myself from those influences and surround myself with people who inspired me—one of them being my longtime friend, Mark. He had always been supportive and encouraged me to pursue my dreams.

Final Thoughts

Your past doesn't define you, but the lessons you take from it can help you create something better. You don't need to be perfect. Just show up for yourself, dare to dream, and take intentional steps toward a life that excites you.

Grab a journal and start visualizing your ideal life. Writing down your thoughts and dreams clarifies your vision and reinforces your commitment to change. Take the first step toward a new goal. Invest in yourself, build resilience, and surround yourself with positivity. Don't just get by—start building something extraordinary. The best part? You're the architect of it all.

The road ahead may not always be smooth, but with resilience and determination, it will lead to a life that truly feels like your own.

Chapter Key Points

- **Shift your mindset.** Stop viewing life as something to endure and start embracing it as an opportunity for growth and fulfillment.

- **Reconnect with your passions.** Rediscover hobbies, interests, and dreams that bring you joy and a sense of purpose.

- **Define clear, achievable goals.** Align them with your values and personal growth.

- **Find joy in everyday moments.** Practice gratitude, mindfulness, and self-care to create a life that feels rich and rewarding.

- **Surround yourself with positive influences.** Take calculated risks and invest in personal development.

- **Use your experiences to support and inspire others.** Building connections with those on similar journeys fosters resilience and growth.

Chapter Seven

Avoiding Common Pitfalls:

What Not to Do in the Recovery Process

"More people would learn from their mistakes if they weren't so busy denying them."
- Harold J. Smith

Moving Forward: Breaking Free from the Past

Going through my divorce pushed me into actions and emotions I never imagined experiencing. At first, I thought it was all just a phase, and I assumed I was processing things in a healthy way. But I was wrong. When I finally stepped back and assessed my reality, I realized I had spent my days binge-watching TV, eating junk food, and avoiding any contact with others.

I thought I was protecting my energy and avoiding unnecessary stress. But in reality, I was building walls. These walls temporarily numbed my emotions and kept the pain at bay, but they also kept me stuck. I avoided people, buried myself in distractions, and mistook isolation for healing. The illusion of safety made me cancel plans and dodge social interactions under the guise of self-preservation. But before I knew it, even simple tasks, like going to the grocery store, felt overwhelming.

I remember standing at my front door, my hand gripping the knob, heart racing at the mere thought of stepping outside. The longer I stayed hidden, the scarier it became to re-enter the world.

Another common illusion is believing that time alone will heal everything. While time plays a role, true healing requires active effort—whether through self-reflection, therapy, or taking deliberate steps to rebuild your life. You might hear others say, "Just give yourself time." But time alone doesn't heal wounds. It's what you do during that time that fosters real healing.

I spent months thinking I was "working on myself," but in reality, I was just rereading old messages from my ex and letting bitterness settle in my mind. Don't get me wrong—it's important to sit with your emotions and process them fully. But wallowing in them without taking steps forward only leads to stagnation.

Another trap is false productivity. You might tell yourself you're making progress, but in reality, you're just avoiding discomfort in new ways. You throw yourself into work or sign up for endless self-help webinars but never apply what you learn. True healing isn't about keeping busy—it's about addressing the emotions beneath the surface.

This chapter will help you recognize the subtle illusions preventing your healing and keeping you stuck. We'll discuss the dangers of isolation, the myths surrounding closure, and how to shift your mindset from waiting to feel better to actively taking steps toward recovery.

The Dangers of Over-Focusing on Your Ex

After a divorce, it's natural for your mind to seek answers. "What could I have done differently? Was it all my fault?" In your search for closure, you might find yourself fixating on your ex—reliving old memories, searching for hidden meanings, or wondering if they've moved on. This isn't a personal weakness; it's a natural response to loss. However, continuously focusing on your ex only drains your energy and slows down your healing process.

Scrolling through their social media, dissecting their every move, or hoping for reconciliation won't give you closure. Instead, it traps you in a never-ending loop of obsession. The more you search, the more questions arise, fueling the cycle further.

To move forward, you need to shift your focus from your ex to yourself. Once you make this shift, you can begin to rebuild your life.

The Brain's Response to Breakups

Three common mental patterns emerge after a breakup: the brain's "broken record" phenomenon, the addiction to closure, and the social media cycle.

1. The Brain's "Broken Record" Phenomenon

When a relationship ends abruptly, your brain replays arguments, memories, and "what-ifs" on repeat. This isn't a sign of weakness—it's your limbic system trying to resolve uncertainty. Neuroscientists refer to this as the "negativity bias," a survival mechanism that prioritizes unresolved pain over neutral or positive thoughts.

In early human history, vigilance against threats was essential for survival. Today, that same instinct kicks in when you face emotional distress, like seeing your ex move on. This response floods your body with stress hormones like cortisol, making the breakup feel like a recurring wound.

A 2019 study showed that ruminating on past relationships activates the same brain regions that process physical pain, making it feel as though you're reliving the breakup repeatedly.

2. The Addiction to "Closure"

Your brain craves closure because it loves neat and tidy endings. You assume that once you get closure, you'll heal faster. But closure is a myth. It isn't something that happens in a single conversation or apology—it's something you create for yourself over time.

Psychologist Dr. Robert Leahy explains that obsession often stems from an inability to handle uncertainty. Developing a tolerance for uncertainty is essential for healing.

It allows you to shift your focus from what you can't control to what you can—your personal growth, mindset, and future. When you feel powerless about the future, your mind clings to the past, seeking answers that may never come.

To truly move forward, you must accept that the future is unpredictable and that your healing doesn't depend on your ex's actions—it depends on your willingness to let go.

3. The Social Media Cycle

Scrolling through your ex's social media activates a dopamine loop. Every refresh brings a fleeting rush of excitement, followed by a crash of regret. This pattern mirrors gambling addiction—occasional "wins" keep you hooked.

A 2021 study found that even a brief glance at an ex's social media profile can increase heart rate and distress by 34%.

Signs You're Over-Focusing on Your Ex

Recognizing when you're fixating on your ex is crucial for personal growth. Without awareness, these habits can prolong emotional distress and prevent you from moving forward.

1. Overanalyzing

You obsess over their new partner's looks, career, or interests. You track their life updates and see them as "proof" that they're thriving without you. This kind of comparison is unfair and harmful—your journey is unique, and healing isn't a race.

2. Replaying the Past

You replay old arguments in your head, imagining the perfect comeback. You dwell on tiny moments and convince yourself they were turning points. A psychological study on counterfactual thinking—imagining "what could have been"—found that this habit increases anxiety and depression by reinforcing feelings of helplessness.

3. Letting Their Actions Control Your Emotions

Your mood hinges on your ex's actions, making it difficult to regain emotional control. Instead, focus on building your emotional stability by engaging in activities that bring you joy, setting personal goals, and establishing boundaries that allow you to move forward independently.

A vague text like "We need to talk" ruins your whole week. A simple profile picture change sends you into a spiral of analysis. Your brain, overwhelmed by emotions, interprets these neutral actions as threats, reinforcing feelings of loss.

How to Shift Your Focus and Heal

Moving on from someone you once loved is never easy. This is someone you cared for deeply and shared so much with. Now that they're no longer in your life, everything feels different, maybe even empty. Your routines, your home, and your daily life all carry reminders of them, making it hard to let go.

But moving forward isn't just about willpower—it's an active process that requires rewiring your thoughts and breaking old emotional habits. Here's how to start making that shift:

Set Boundaries

Protecting your peace starts with setting clear boundaries. These boundaries help reduce your exposure to emotional triggers and can significantly lower stress levels in just a few weeks.

Start by taking a digital detox. Unfollow, mute, or block your ex on social media. If you need to stay in touch for co-parenting reasons, use apps like OurFamilyWizard to keep conversations focused on logistics rather than emotions.

If you receive a text from your ex or hear something about them, wait at least a few hours before responding—except in emergencies. Giving your brain time to process will help you respond logically instead of emotionally.

Redirect Your Energy

Research from the American Psychological Association has shown that being physically active increases dopamine levels, enhancing mood and promoting overall well-being. For example, a 2018 study found that just 30 minutes of moderate exercise can significantly reduce stress and improve emotional resilience.

So, when you catch yourself thinking about your ex, change your environment. Step outside, splash water on your face or do 10 jumping jacks. These small actions interrupt the cycle of obsession.

Engage in activities that require complete focus, like watching a new TV show, learning an instrument, or solving a puzzle. These "flow" activities quiet your default mode network (DMN), the part of your brain responsible for overthinking and self-doubt.

Practice Compassionate Detachment

Psychologist Kristin Neff's research on self-compassion shows that treating yourself with kindness rather than self-criticism reduces overthinking and speeds up emotional recovery.

To be compassionate to yourself, write a "release" letter. Pour out everything you feel—your hurt, anger, and hopes for what could have been. Then, burn or bury it. This symbolic act tells your mind it's time to let go.

After burning the letter, take a moment to acknowledge the emotional release it provides. This act symbolizes letting go of the past, allowing you to shift your mindset. Reframe your thoughts by replacing self-doubt and regret with self-growth and lessons learned. Instead of asking, "Why did they leave?" try, "What did this relationship teach me about myself?" This helps you focus on growth instead of pain.

The Power of Small Shifts

Healing doesn't happen overnight. It's a journey filled with emotional ups and downs, moments of progress, and occasional setbacks. Some days will feel easier than others, while some will challenge your strength. But with patience and persistence, each small step forward contributes to lasting emotional growth.

You can't go from loving someone wholeheartedly to forgetting about their existence in a day. Take things slowly. Change what you can, bit by bit. The small shifts you make daily might seem insignificant, but over time, they add up to the healing you desire. Here are a few exercises to help:

The 5-Minute Mindfulness Fix

Mindfulness reduces fear and increases your ability to think clearly. Studies in psychology show that as little as eight weeks of mindfulness practice can shrink the amygdala (the fear center of the brain) and strengthen the prefrontal cortex (the rational part of the brain).

So, when obsessive thoughts about your ex arise, set a timer for five minutes and focus solely on your breathing. If your mind wanders, acknowledge the thought as just a thought and bring your focus back to your breath.

Build a "Distraction Menu"

Engaging your senses keeps you in the present and prevents overthinking. Make a list of 10 activities that involve your senses, such as journaling, sketching, painting, or gardening. Whenever thoughts of your ex arise, choose an activity from your list to do immediately.

Leverage Neuroplasticity with Gratitude

Before bed, write down three things you're grateful for that have nothing to do with your ex. This practice gradually rewires your brain to focus on positivity, helping shift your mindset from loss to appreciation for the present moment. Simple things like a warm shower, a friend's weird laugh, or a good book can make a difference. This gratitude practice boosts serotonin levels in your brain and reduces activity in the anterior cingulate cortex, which is associated with emotional pain.

Rebound Relationships: How to Avoid the Cycle

Rebound relationships are like fast food—quick, convenient, and temporarily satisfying, but ultimately lacking the nourishment needed for true emotional healing. They may fill the emptiness for a moment but leave you emotionally drained. In contrast, true healing is like a slow-cooked meal—it takes time, patience, and the right ingredients.

Why the Urge to Rebound is Natural

The urge to jump into a new relationship right after divorce is a common response rooted in emotional and neurological patterns. It doesn't mean that you've always hated your ex or that you're a failure—it's simply your brain seeking comfort and connection during a time of emotional upheaval. When you feel lonely and rejected, your brain craves connection like a thirsty plant craves water. But behind that craving is a complex interplay of emotions and neurochemistry.

The Brain's Panic Button

Divorce can trigger what psychologists call "attachment system activation." Because your brain is designed to bond with others, losing a partner feels like a threat to your survival. This turns on your amygdala, the part of your brain that handles fear, and releases stress hormones like cortisol and adrenaline. Meanwhile, the part of your brain responsible for rational decision-making, the prefrontal cortex, takes a back seat. This is why rebound relationships can feel so urgent, even when your logical side knows you should slow down.

Research has found that rejection activates the same brain regions as physical pain. To cope with that pain, your brain seeks quick relief by forming new romantic connections that release dopamine (the "reward" chemical) and oxytocin (the "bonding" hormone). This temporary high masks your true emotional pain and creates a cycle where you keep seeking that rush.

The Myth of the "Upgrade"

Many rebound relationships stem from a need to prove your worth to yourself, your ex, or even society. Seeking external validation in this way can create a cycle where you repeatedly enter relationships to affirm your desirability rather than to build genuine emotional connections. This often results in attracting partners who fulfill a temporary need rather than contributing to long-term emotional growth.

A study on personal relationships found that people who entered a new relationship within three months of a breakup experienced 52% more emotional distress a year later compared to those who took time to heal.

The 'Ghosts of Relationships Past'

If you haven't fully processed your divorce, unresolved pain will resurface. You may unconsciously choose partners who replicate familiar relationship dynamics because they feel safe, even if they're harmful.

Signs You're in a Rebound Trap

Take some time to reflect and ask yourself if your new relationship is genuinely growing or if it's just your way of avoiding grief. Here are some warning signs:

- You find yourself comparing your new partner to your ex, even in small ways like, "At least they don't snore!"

- You prioritize looks or status over values and emotional connection.

- Your emotions fluctuate wildly depending on the highs and lows of the relationship.

- You feel uneasy when alone and rely on constant communication for distraction.

- You quickly escalate the relationship, rushing through major milestones like saying "I love you" or moving in together.

- You overshare your traumas or depend on your new partner as an emotional therapist.

How to Avoid the Rebound Cycle

Focus on Self-Healing

Commit to 6 to 12 months without dating, giving your mind and heart the space they need to heal. When you jump into a relationship too soon, you risk carrying unresolved baggage into it. A break allows your brain to recalibrate through neuroplasticity—the brain's ability to rewire itself.

Writing can help process emotions. Studies show that just 15 minutes of reflective journaling a day can significantly lower activity in the amygdala. Consider journaling with prompts like:

- What did my marriage teach me about my needs in a relationship?

- What patterns do I fear repeating in my next relationship?

- What kind of love do I truly want to experience moving forward?

Use this time to explore new interests, travel, or engage in hobbies you never had time for before. Investing in yourself creates a fulfilling life without needing external validation.

Set Emotional Boundaries

If you feel drawn to someone new, wait at least 48 hours before acting on it. Ask yourself: Am I truly interested in this person, or am I just trying to avoid loneliness? Give yourself time to reflect before making impulsive decisions.

Before entering a new relationship, ensure you've passed these three checkpoints:

1. **No hidden agenda** – You're not dating to make your ex jealous, prove a point, or "win" the breakup. Your motivation should stem from genuine readiness, not revenge or insecurity.

2. **Emotional independence** – You can spend time alone without feeling the need for constant distractions. If solitude still feels unbearable, it's a sign you need more time to heal.

3. **Clarity on non-negotiables** – You have taken the time to define what truly matters in a relationship (e.g., trust, emotional safety, communication).

Enjoy Being By Yourself

One of the best things about spending time alone is that it teaches you self-love. By embracing solitude, you gain a deeper understanding of your needs, strengths, and boundaries, which helps foster healthier relationships in the future. You deserve love that comes from a place of wholeness, not desperation. Trust the process—and most importantly, trust yourself.

True healing comes when you can be by yourself and still feel whole. Here are some exercises that can help:

- **Dopamine Detox** – For 30 days, avoid activities that give you quick dopamine rushes, like dating apps and flirty texts. Instead, focus on natural mood boosters like cold showers, which have been shown to spike dopamine levels by 250%.

- **Daily Affirmations** – Every morning, look in the mirror and say: "I am enough, with or without a partner." Neuroscience shows that self-affirmations lower stress and strengthen the brain's ability to build self-worth. Repeating positive affirmations daily can rewire neural pathways, fostering greater self-acceptance and emotional resilience.

- **Solo Adventures** – Get comfortable with your own company. Start small—have coffee at a café without your phone, take yourself out to dinner, or go on a solo trip or nature walk. Over time, these experiences will build self-sufficiency and confidence.

- **Build Strong Friendships** – Having friendships outside of romantic relationships boosts oxytocin, the "bonding" hormone. Instead of relying on a new partner to fill the void, join a book club, volunteer, or take a fitness class. Surround yourself with people who support your growth.

Using Substance Abuse or Other Escape Mechanisms as Coping Tools

Wanting to escape emotional pain isn't a sign of weakness—it's a natural survival instinct. Seeking relief is normal, but the key is choosing healthy coping mechanisms that support long-term healing rather than temporary numbness. When grief or stress overwhelms you, your brain looks for quick ways to calm down. However, what starts as temporary relief can turn into a cycle that prevents true healing.

When you're in pain, your amygdala senses a threat and floods your body with stress hormones. To counteract this, your prefrontal cortex (the rational part of your brain) seeks quick relief. Activities like drinking, binge-watching, or emotional eating release dopamine, creating an illusion of comfort.

Stress makes your brain extra sensitive to dopamine, amplifying the appeal of distractions and making it harder to break free from the escape cycle. This heightened sensitivity reinforces cravings for quick relief, keeping you trapped in a pattern of avoidance. This creates a loop that looks like this: **Pain □ Escape □ Dopamine Hit □ Craving More Escape.**

You might tell yourself, "Just one drink," or "I'll stop scrolling after 10 minutes." But these escape mechanisms often lead to a loss of control. This phenomenon is called the **"what-the-hell effect."** Once you lose control, guilt kicks in, making you want to escape even more.

Research in *Addictive Behaviors* shows that people who use alcohol to manage stress are **four times more likely** to develop dependency compared to social drinkers. This happens because the brain starts to associate relief with the substance.

Even non-substance escapes like overworking, mindless scrolling, or emotional eating prevent you from processing your emotions. True healing doesn't come from numbing pain—it comes from facing and working through it.

Signs You Might Be Escaping

Not all coping mechanisms are helpful. If you're unsure whether yours is helping or harming you, pay attention to these signs:

1. The Numbness Cycle

With this cycle, you rely on distractions or substances to shut off your emotions. When you lie in bed at night, it feels unbearable unless you have something to numb you. Over time, avoiding emotions shrinks the **hippocampus**, the part of the brain responsible for emotional regulation, making it even harder to manage stress.

2. Using Isolation as a Shield

You might find yourself canceling plans to stay home and engage in your escape habit. Conversations with others start to feel exhausting because you're avoiding your true feelings. Social withdrawal activates the brain's **default mode network**, which fuels overthinking and depression.

3. The Guilt-Avoidance Loop

You wake up determined to change, but by the afternoon, you've already slipped back into old habits. When this happens, shame convinces you that since you've already "failed," you might as well keep going. This only strengthens the cycle of avoidance.

How to Break Free from Escaping

To break free, try these evidence-based strategies:

1. Therapy and Counseling

Cognitive Behavioral Therapy (**CBT**) helps identify triggers and replace negative thought patterns. Group therapy is also effective—it connects you with others who share similar struggles, reducing feelings of shame and isolation.

2. Physical Activity

Aerobic activities like running, swimming, or dancing release **endorphins**, which reduce stress and provide the same comforting effect as dopamine. Mindful practices like **yoga or tai chi** have also been shown to **reduce stress hormones by 31%**, making them great alternatives to unhealthy coping habits.

3. Mindfulness Practices

Practicing mindful meditation for just **eight weeks** can shrink the amygdala and strengthen the prefrontal cortex, improving emotional regulation. The **RAIN technique** is another helpful way to process emotions:

- **Recognize** what you're feeling.

- **Allow** it to exist without judgment.

- **Investigate** how it feels in your body.

- **Nurture** yourself with kindness.

Another mindful practice is **"Morning Pages."** Every morning, write three pages of unfiltered thoughts. This clears your mind and helps release emotions.

Navigating Recovery with Accountability

Accountability plays a key role in breaking free from unhealthy coping mechanisms. Here's how you can stay on track:

1. Track Your Habits

Use a simple notebook or an app to log what triggers your urge to escape. Is it loneliness? Conflict? Stress? Then, note what **healthy coping mechanism** you tried instead. Reviewing your progress each week helps you recognize patterns and celebrate small victories.

2. Build a Support System

Your support system makes all the difference. Have **two or three people** who can check in on you without judgment. Be clear in your requests, such as: *"Can I text you when I feel the urge to numb out?"* If you prefer structured support, programs like **SMART Recovery** or **Refuge Recovery** combine science with community to break unhealthy coping cycles.

3. Acknowledge Small Daily Wins

Saying, *"I went for a walk instead of opening a bottle of wine,"* or *"I called a friend instead of scrolling through my ex's social media,"* reinforces positive changes. These small wins strengthen your resolve to keep making healthier choices.

The Road to Long-Term Healing

Progress won't always be straight and smooth. **Setbacks are a natural part of healing, and it's important to practice self-compassion.** Instead of seeing them as failures, view them as opportunities to learn and grow. Prepare for setbacks—old habits may resurface, and some days will feel harder than others. But each time you choose a healthy response, you choose yourself. Over time, your brain will start focusing more on your future than your past.

Chapter Key Points

- **Break free from unhealthy thought loops** and stop fixating on your ex. Focus on your own growth instead of dwelling on the past.

- **Don't isolate yourself.** Stay connected with supportive friends, family, or a community to prevent loneliness and negative self-talk.

- **Give yourself time to heal** before jumping into a new relationship out of loneliness or insecurity. Resist rushing into a rebound.

- **Manage stress in healthy ways** and avoid destructive coping mechanisms like excessive drinking, overeating, or reckless spending.

- **Shift from blaming circumstances to taking ownership** of your healing.

- **Embrace new experiences, perspectives, and challenges** instead of clinging to old habits or comfort zones. Stay open to change.

Chapter Eight

Living Your Best Life Post-Divorce:

Life After Wife

"It is never too late to be what you might have been."

- George Eliot

Moving Forward with Intention

Have you ever felt like you're wearing a mask, pretending everything is fine while struggling inside? You put on a brave face, acting as though you've moved on, but deep down, are you being honest with yourself? True healing isn't about rushing the process—it's about moving forward slowly and with intention.

This is your chance to redefine what love and success truly mean to you. It's an opportunity to surround yourself with the right people and create a fulfilling life. Many call this the recovery phase, but I like to think of it as the transformation phase. Seeing it as a transformation shifts the focus from pain to possibility, from what was lost to what can be gained. This perspective fosters resilience by encouraging you to view challenges as opportunities for personal growth and renewal, helping you move forward with purpose and optimism.

Once the dust settles and the paperwork is finalized, you're left with a blank slate. What you do with it is entirely up to you. Will you create a better life, or will you remain stuck replaying what could have been?

This chapter is about showing you how to move forward with confidence. I'll share the tools that helped me become a better person, and I hope they will be just as valuable to you. Once you discover this light, don't keep it to yourself—share it with others on the same journey.

Navigating the Emotional Shift

You're sitting in a cozy café, a warm cup of coffee in your hands, watching the world go by. You see couples laughing and friends deep in conversation, and for a moment, you wonder if you'll ever feel that happy again.

After a divorce, it's normal to feel lost. You might experience a whirlwind of emotions—grief, anger, relief, loneliness, or even guilt. It's a time of transition where everything familiar changes, and it's easy to question who you are without your partner. I felt the same way. Going from being coupled to being single can feel like an uphill battle.

Regaining confidence after divorce doesn't happen overnight, but it does happen. You're retraining your mind to live without someone you once loved, and that's a challenge. So, take your time and stay consistent. The life you desire will find you. Now, let's discuss rebuilding your lost confidence.

Steps to Rebuild Your Confidence

1. Redefine Success on Your Terms

After divorce, society pressures you to follow a certain script—start dating again, find someone new, and "move on." But true success after divorce isn't about meeting external expectations. It's about defining fulfillment on your own terms. What do you truly want?

For me, success started with something as simple as my morning routine. Instead of reaching for my phone first thing or sinking into sadness, I made a habit of going for a walk, journaling and enjoying a good cup of coffee. This small practice gave me a sense of control over my own life.

Take some time to reflect on what success means for you. Maybe it's not tied to a career or finding a new relationship. What if true success lies in feeling at peace in your own company or revisiting a hobby you used to love? Whatever it is, let it be yours alone.

2. Embrace the Power of Yet

One of the most powerful mindset shifts I made was adding a single word to how I talk: *yet*. For example, I used to say, "I don't know how to start over," and it felt like a final statement, reinforcing my fears. But when I changed it to, "I don't know how to start over... yet," it left room for growth. That small shift helped me take action, step by step until I realized that change was possible.

For the longest time, I told myself: "I'm not happy. I don't feel strong. I can't see a future I'm excited about." But when I started saying: "I'm not happy... yet. I don't feel strong... yet. I can't see a future I'm excited about... yet," everything changed.

That one word reminded me that feelings aren't permanent. I wasn't stuck; I was evolving. And so are you. Just because you don't feel confident today doesn't mean you won't tomorrow or in the weeks to come. Be kind to yourself—step by step, choice by choice, and win by win. Confidence is still possible.

3. Start Your Day with Affirmations

At first, I was skeptical about affirmations. Saying positive things about myself felt weird, almost forced. But I decided to give it a try. Every morning, I wrote down three affirmations: "I am worthy," "I am stronger than I think," and "I am capable of creating a life I love."

At first, the words felt empty, but over time, they started to sink in. Slowly, they replaced self-doubt with self-belief. If you're struggling to trust in yourself, start with just one affirmation. Write it down, say it out loud, and repeat it daily. In time, you'll begin to believe it.

4. Step Outside Your Comfort Zone

One of the best ways to build confidence is to do something that scares you. For me, that meant signing up for a local art class. I hesitated at first. I wasn't a great artist and thought I'd feel out of place. But once I stepped into that classroom, I realized everyone was there for the same reason: to learn and create. Nobody cared how good I was. They were just focused on their growth.

By the end of the class, I didn't become a pro artist, but I felt lighter and more energized. The real victory wasn't in the painting I created but in proving to myself that I could try something new.

5. Cultivate a Supportive Environment

In the early stages of my divorce, I made the mistake of isolating myself. I ignored calls, avoided social gatherings, and convinced myself that I had to figure things out alone. But the more I withdrew, the more stuck I felt. Eventually, I started reaching out. I texted old friends, joined a book club, and even saw a therapist. Every interaction reminded me that I wasn't alone.

Support doesn't always mean deep conversations about your struggles. Sometimes, it's just laughing over coffee or feeling seen by someone who understands. The energy around you plays a huge role in how you see yourself. So, surround yourself with people who make you happy.

Continuing the Journey of Self-Improvement

Turning a New Page After Divorce

After a divorce, everything can feel like a loss. Your routine is disrupted, your sense of stability is shaken, and emotions like grief, loneliness, and uncertainty can feel over-whelming. The future seems unclear, and even the version of yourself you once knew may feel unfamiliar. But as time passes, a shift begins. You realize that this isn't just an ending—it's also a beginning. A blank slate. A time to redefine who you are and who you want to become.

I once had a neighbor who felt completely lost when his marriage ended. He had been stuck in a job he didn't love, and at first, divorce felt like yet another blow. But as he sat with his new reality, he saw it as something else—an opportunity. Instead of staying stuck, he enrolled in a digital marketing course.

Through the course, he met people who had overcome similar struggles and found a new purpose. Their stories motivated him to push past his own doubts and take action. He realized that change was within his control and that by stepping outside of his comfort zone, he could create a future that felt fulfilling and meaningful. More than anything, he proved to himself that he wasn't trapped in his past.

That's the beauty of self-improvement—it allows you to take control of your growth, rediscover your potential, and build a life that feels fulfilling. Self-improvement is a lifelong journey, and this time, you're doing it for yourself. Not for a partner, not to fit into a role, but because you deserve a life that excites you.

Lifelong Learning and Growth

There's a common misconception that growth happens in big leaps. But in reality, growth is built in the small choices we make every day. For me, the first step toward growth after my divorce wasn't a massive change—it was something simple.

I picked up a book. Not just any book, but one about a topic I had always been curious about but never prioritized: philosophy. As I flipped through the pages, something clicked. I realized how much time I had spent looking back at my past instead of feeding my mind with something new.

That decision to learn sparked something in me. I started watching documentaries, jotting down ideas that inspired me, and eventually signing up for online courses—not because I had to, but because I wanted to. Learning reignited my curiosity and reminded me that life still had more to offer.

Exploring New Hobbies

There's something exciting about trying something for the first time as an adult. You're no longer doing it for a grade, for someone's approval, or to meet expectations. You're doing it purely for the experience itself.

For me, that thing was woodworking. During my marriage, I had always been focused on practical tasks. I fixed things around the house but never truly built something from scratch. After my divorce, I decided to take on a project. I bought some tools, watched tutorials, and slowly started creating things out of wood.

The first piece wasn't perfect, but the process itself was incredibly satisfying. I wasn't aiming to become an expert craftsman—I wanted to prove to myself that I could learn, create, and enjoy my own company in the process.

Hobbies do more than pass the time. They keep your mind engaged, provide a creative outlet, and remind you that life is meant to be experienced, not just endured. Whatever interests you, start and let yourself get lost in it.

Investing in Education

One of the biggest realizations I had after my divorce was how much of my future was still unwritten. The dreams I had shelved, the interests I had ignored, and the goals I had put on hold were suddenly within reach again. For the first time in years, I had the freedom to pursue them on my terms.

I rediscovered my passion for writing, something I had once loved but had set aside. I started journaling again, then moved on to creative writing, and before I knew it, I was working on a book—something I never thought possible before.

Education doesn't have to mean going back to school. It can be as simple as taking an online course in a subject you've always been curious about, attending a seminar or workshop to develop a skill that could improve your career, or reading books that give you new ideas.

For me, it was taking a personal finance course. I had always been somewhat passive when it came to money. But after my divorce, I knew I needed to take control of my financial future. The more I learned, the more empowered I felt. That's the power of knowledge—it builds confidence and reminds you that you're capable of so much more than you ever realized.

Practicing Emotional Resilience

Self-improvement isn't just about achieving more; it's about understanding yourself better. Emotional resilience became one of the most important skills I developed after my divorce.

I remember one day when I found myself wallowing in my negative thoughts again. Instead of pushing those feelings away, I decided to face them. I sat down with my journal, wrote out everything I was feeling, and practiced being kind to myself. And you know what? It helped a lot.

Emotional resilience means knowing how to handle pain when it comes. It's about recognizing your emotions, understanding what triggers them, and learning healthy coping strategies like journaling, therapy, or mindfulness. It also means building a support system that encourages you to keep moving forward.

The more you prioritize your emotional well-being, the stronger you'll feel in every part of your life. So, wake up each day and ask yourself: *What can I learn today? How can I take one step forward?*

Offering Advice to Fellow Men Going Through Divorce

Healing Through Connection

When I first went through my divorce, I felt completely alone in my pain. It seemed like my struggle was mine alone. But over time, I began to open up and have honest conversations with other men who had been through similar challenges. That's when I discovered something powerful: we heal better when we heal together.

There's an old saying, "The best way to learn something is to teach it." When it comes to divorce recovery, this couldn't be more true. You don't need to be an expert, therapist, or life coach to support another man going through this. All you need to do is say, *"I've been there, and I understand."*

Sharing your journey not only helps others but also reminds you of your strength. During a divorce, you're mostly just trying to survive. But as you start to move forward, you begin to see what mistakes to avoid, what strategies helped, and what you wish you had done differently. That knowledge is valuable to others who are still in the divorce process.

You can become someone's mentor, whether through structured support like a formal group or informal conversations over coffee. Mentorship doesn't require having all the answers—it's about being present, offering encouragement, and reminding others that healing is possible. When I first stepped into mentorship, I didn't realize how much I would gain in return. A friend going through a separation reached out to me, unsure of what to do next. We met for coffee, and I just listened. He wasn't looking for immediate solutions—he just needed to hear, *"Yeah, man, I've been there too."* That conversation led to more check-ins, shared advice, and the realization that by helping him, I was also reinforcing my own growth.

Ways to Support Other Men Going Through Divorce

Supporting other men going through a divorce is one of the most rewarding ways to help someone else heal. By offering guidance and encouragement, you not only provide comfort to others but also reinforce your own healing journey. Helping others allows you to reflect on your progress, solidify the lessons you've learned, and build a sense of purpose beyond your own struggles. When you help someone else, you break the cycle of isolation and remind fellow men that they're not alone in their struggles.

1. Join or Create a Support Group

Men often face societal pressure to suppress their emotions, making it difficult to find healthy outlets for processing feelings. We're taught to tough it out, move on, and not dwell on emotions. But divorce shatters that idea! You have to process it, or it will eat you alive.

That's why support groups, whether formal or informal, are important. They provide a space for men to talk openly, get advice, and hear from others who understand. When I first joined a small support group, I was nervous and skeptical. I expected it to be awkward. Instead, I left that first meeting feeling much lighter. I realized that there were other men at various stages of their journey who could offer advice and encouragement.

If you aren't comfortable with being in a formal group, you can support others in different ways. Talk to a coworker who's struggling, reach out to an old friend, or even connect with someone online. Offering a listening ear, sharing your own experiences, or simply checking in with someone who might be having a tough time can make a significant difference.

2. Lead by Example

Sometimes, simply living your life is the most powerful message. When you show that divorce isn't the end of life but rather a new beginning, others will notice. So, engage in self-care, focus on your career, and show up for your kids—your actions speak volumes.

When I began working to rebuild my life, other men started asking me questions: *"How did you get through those first few months?"* or *"What helped you when you felt stuck?"* These conversations were never lectures, just honest discussions between men who wanted to heal.

If you're not comfortable giving advice, that's okay. Simply living a life you're proud of can inspire others more than you know.

3. Share Practical Advice

Emotional support is essential, but sometimes men need straightforward, practical guidance. This could mean sharing financial tips, offering help with co-parenting challenges, or directing someone to resources that helped you.

For instance, I remember feeling overwhelmed by all the paperwork after my divorce—legal forms, financial documents, custody agreements, and everything else. I spent weeks sorting through it all. Later, when a friend faced the same struggle, I shared a simple checklist I had created. That small gesture saved him hours of stress.

Practical advice can be as simple as:

- Learning how to create a budget after divorce

- Sharing useful apps for managing shared custody

- Recommending books, podcasts, or articles that helped you

I even knew someone who started a blog after his divorce as a way to process his feelings. At first, he felt like he was shouting into the void, but soon, other men began to read his posts, leave comments, and share their own experiences. His blog turned into a small but powerful community where men could exchange advice, vent frustrations, and remind each other that healing was possible.

Fostering Community, Connection, and Ongoing Self-Care

Healing can be messy, but it's easier when you don't go through it alone. After divorce, it's all too easy to feel like you're stumbling through life. But the real work starts when you connect with others and truly take care of yourself.

1. Finding Your People (Community)

Building a community is more than just joining a group. It involves finding people who get it. Some old friendships may change, but that leaves space for new ones. Reach out to that friend you lost touch with, join a local group, or be open to conversations with those who share your struggles.

2. Meaningful Relationships (Connection)

Meaningful relationships aren't always about romance. Sometimes, the strongest bonds come from friendships, family ties, or even a mentor who's been through similar battles. These relationships remind you that you're not alone and that someone truly understands what you're going through.

3. Keeping Yourself Strong (Self-Care)

Finally, remember self-care. Divorce takes a toll on both your body and mind. Regular exercise, mindfulness, and even therapy aren't just trendy ideas—they will keep you grounded. You can't pour from an empty cup; when you take care of yourself, you're better equipped to support others as well.

Final Thoughts

Life after divorce is more than just getting through each day—you must create a life worth waking up to. Every time you share your story, support a friend, or take a moment for yourself, you prove that you are stronger than your struggles.

Your raw, unfiltered truth matters, and by living it, you can inspire others to do the same. So, keep it real. Embrace the messiness, lean on those who understand, and allow others to lean on you for strength.

Chapter Key Points

- Shift your focus from what you've lost to what you can create, and celebrate small wins along the way.

- Explore new hobbies, invest in education, and commit to lifelong growth.

- Share your experiences, mentor fellow men, and build a community of support.

- Prioritize meaningful connections—relationships that uplift and inspire you.

- Take care of your well-being through self-care, mindfulness, and healthy habits.

- Define success on your own terms, building a life that aligns with your values, passions, and goals—not societal expectations.

Chapter Nine

Final Words

CONGRATULATIONS! YOU'VE NOW REACHED the end of this book. This journey was never just about moving on—it was about rediscovering your strength, reclaiming your identity, and stepping into a future filled with possibility. I commend you for your dedication and commitment to your personal growth.

Before I leave you to start implementing all you've learned, I want to leave you with a few final thoughts.

Divorce is a turning point, not a limitation—let it be the catalyst for transformation, growth, and a future that reflects your true self. Use this moment to explore new passions, strengthen your personal relationships, or even pursue a career change that aligns with your true values. Each challenge presents an opportunity to rebuild your life in a way that feels authentic and fulfilling. Instead of seeing divorce as the end of your story, embrace it as the close of one chapter and the beginning of another.

As you've seen throughout this journey, healing, growth, and rediscovery are possible. You have the power to shape your future in a way that reflects your values, passions, and dreams.

Moving Forward with Purpose

Don't rush this new journey to meet anyone else's expectations. Set personal goals that align with your vision, not what others expect from you, and allow yourself the time and space to grow at your own pace. Remember why you picked up this book in the first place. Learn from your past and embrace your future with an open heart.

Be courageous and take bold steps, no matter how small. Every action you take lays the foundation for a stronger, wiser, and more fulfilled version of yourself. Growth happens in increments, and each step forward brings you closer to the life you envision.

You Are Not Alone

Most importantly, you're not alone. Millions of men have walked this path before you, and countless others are navigating it now. The strength of community and shared experiences can make all the difference. Lean on those who uplift you, and when you're ready, offer the same support to others who are beginning their journey.

If this book has resonated with you, I encourage you to share your experience with others. Your story could be the encouragement someone else needs to begin their healing journey. Recommend this book to those who may find value in it and contribute to a larger community of understanding and support.

Together, we can redefine what it means to live a fulfilling life after divorce.

A New Beginning

Take a deep breath and look forward. Embrace the journey ahead with confidence, knowing that each choice you make shapes your future. Challenges may come, but with each hurdle crossed, you'll find the strength and clarity to overcome. The road ahead is yours to create.

Cheers to new beginnings, brighter days, and the unshakable belief that your best days are yet to come.

Best Wishes!

If you enjoyed reading *Divorce for Men: Rebuilding Your Life After Wife*, I'd really appreciate it if you could take a moment to leave a review. Your feedback not only helps me but also makes it easier for other men going through similar challenges to find the book. Honest reviews—whether short or detailed—go a long way in spreading the word and supporting those who need it most. Thank you for your time and support!

FOR USA REVIEW

US - https://bit.ly/4bj0fzl

FOR AUSTRALIA REVIEW

Australia - https://bit.ly/438N aXl

FOR CANADA REVIEW

*Canada - https://bit.ly/4gSe7
C5*

FOR UK REVIEW

UK - https://bit.ly/3ETE5aR

References

AmericanPsychological Association. (2013, April). Marriage and divorce: Changes and challenges. APA Monitor on Psychology. Retrieved from https://www.apa.or g/monitor/2013/04/marriage

AmericanPsychological Association. (2023, November). Navigating late-in-life di vorce.APA Monitor on Psychology. Retrieved from https://www.apa.org/monito r/2023/11/navigating-late-in-life-divorce

Blocker, E.(n.d.). Reclaim your life after divorce. LinkedIn. Retrieved from https: //www.linkedin.com/pulse/reclaim-your-life-after-divorce-erica-blocker-m-a-cpc

Claire MacklinCoaching. (2019, January 9). Five ways to take back your power after divorce.Claire Macklin Coaching Blog. Retrieved from https://www.clairemackli ncoaching.com/blog-1/2019/1/9/five-ways-to-take-back-your-power

Girltalk HQ.(n.d.). From pain to power: My journey from divorce to empowerment. Retrieved from https://www.girltalkhq.com/from-pain-to-power-my-journey-fro m-divorce-to-empowerment/

Grice, J. (n.d.).Reclaiming your life after divorce. Retrieved from https://jengrice .com/reclaiming-your-life-after-divorce/

Kate Anthony.(2024). Drop the rope: Embracing your power during divorce [Pod cast]. TheDivorce Survival Guide Podcast. Retrieved from https://kateanthony.c om/podcast/episode-296-drop-the-rope-embracing-your-power-during-divorce/

Madrid, J.(n.d.). A positive mindset is a powerful tool for navigating change. Link edIn.Retrieved from https://www.linkedin.com/posts/jimmadrid_a-positive-min dset-is-a-powerful-tool-that-activity-7183117231470358530-49N0

Main Line DivorceMediator. (n.d.). How to reclaim your power after divorce. Healthy DivorceBlog. Retrieved from https://www.mainlinedivorcemediator.com /healthy-divorce-blog/how-to-reclaim-your-power

Miller Law Group.(n.d.). Reclaiming your power after a divorce you didn't choose [Pod cast].Miller Law. Retrieved from https://miller-law.com/podcast/reclaiming-your-pow er-after-a-divorce-you-didnt-choose/

National Centerfor Biotechnology Information. (n.d.). Divorce and its psychological effects.PMC. Retrieved from https://pmc.ncbi.nlm.nih.gov/articles/PMC3132556/

Petrelli Law.(2022). Divorce statistics for 2022. Retrieved from https://www.petrellila w.com/divorce-statistics-for-2022/

Signs Magazine.(2025, January). Five things I learned from my divorce. Retrieved from https://signsmag.com/2025/01/five-things-i-learned-from-my-divorce/

Sonya, N. (n.d.).How to reclaim your life after a breakup or a divorce and turn it into an opportunity. Medium. Retrieved from https://medium.com/@sonyan_65563/how-to-reclaim-your-life-after-a-breakup -or-a-divorce-and-turn-it-into-an-opportunity-149282de807b

Separ8. (n.d.).How to heal and start rebuilding your life after divorce. Retrieved from ht tps://separ8.co.uk/tips-advice/how-to-heal-and-start-rebuilding-your-life-after-divorce/

Made in the USA
Las Vegas, NV
02 April 2025

5cc28875-0e70-4358-ad11-48e103fc27d4R01